Contents

Preface / *4*

Lore of the Land / *8*

On the Road / *19*

Lots of Limericks / *28*

Full Coarse Meals / *42*

The Other Place / *48*

Laughing Matters / *54*

Officious Notices / *71*

Rhymes & Reasons / *77*

Mad Ads / *92*

The World of Business / *98*

Our Graffiti / *104*

Bumpers & Buttons / *111*

From See to Saw / *115*

The Last Word / *132*

Preface

No doubt it is too much to claim that this collection of unexpected wit and unintentional humour makes a significant statement about what Carl Sandburg has called "the people, the bookless people." But it might not be too much to claim that the wit and humour in this little book, almost all of which is appearing in print for the first time anywhere, does add to the gaiety of nations — or at least to the gaiety of a single nation, Canada. That, certainly, is its aim.

Here are bloopers, bumper-stickers, epitaphs, funny letters, graffiti, howlers, jingles, lapel buttons, limericks, malaprops, memos, misprints, puns, rhymes and road signs aplenty. It's all amusing material and it comes from St. John's, Nfld., in the East, to Victoria, B.C., in the West; from Inuvik, N.W.T., in the North, to Windsor, Ont., in the South; and from scores of points that lie between. One might ask how a single editor or lone compiler could amass so much anonymous humour, all of it Canadian in origin. There is an answer to that question.

Colombo's Little Book is really the first supplement to the mammoth quote book that appeared in 1974 as *Colombo's Canadian Quotations*. When I started collecting Canadian quotations, I discovered that the entries were of two types, the "heavy" and the "light." The "heavy" category included familiar and memorable remarks made by Canadians about any subject as well as observations made by foreigners about Canada. The "light" category included anonymous material that, while of no historic interest, possessed much human interest and considerable charm all its own. To shine, all it needed was the proper setting. From the first I visualized it forming "a collection of anonymous humorous ephemera."

Colombo's Little Book of Canadian Proverbs, Graffiti, Limericks & Other Vital Matters;

Compiled by John Robert Colombo;

Illustrations by Peter Whalley & David J. Shaw;

Published by Hurtig Publishers, Edmonton.

**This book is for
Theodore, Catherine, Jonathan**

Copyright © 1975 by J. R. Colombo
All rights reserved
Hurtig Publishers
10560 105 Street
Edmonton, Alberta
ISBN 0-88830-092-1

Printed and bound in Canada

Then the "light" category increased dramatically in size. A national newspaper supplement ran an article on my quote-collecting project, and eight hundred readers responded with almost one thousand examples of "light" humour. Then a morning radio program ran a contest inviting Toronto listeners to submit their favourite pieces of anonymous material, and I received one hundred and fifty more specimens. The material from these two sources fills two-thirds of the pages here. The rest of the material I either spotted myself (it is amazing how observant one can be if one has a purpose in mind, and a pencil and paper handy) or gleaned from out-of-the-way books and out-of-print publications devoted to Canada, a half-historic, half-storied land.

There is a poetic dimension to the contents of this book. Like a work of art, some of the items of wit and humour will give the reader a "lift," an unexpected insight into a situation. They do so through the medium of words — through a marvellous economy of words. We are governed by syllables, somebody once said, and this collection of pithy expressions shows the degree to which we rely on words for our sense of appropriateness and well-being. A slight incongruity or unexpectedness in the word order breaks the pattern of thought. It is too much to claim that the material here represents "the poetry of the people," or "an everyday art," but much in this collection is of both sub-literary and sociological interest.

One wonders what a cultural historian in the twenty-first century (a specialist, let us say, in early- or post-Canadian studies) would make of this collection of humorous ephemera. He might observe that Canadians, in their automobiles, are inveterate speeders, or that in their restaurants they are used to pretentious menus. He might note our obsession with elimination and salvation. He might decide we were a malicious yet witty lot. Closing the book he might speculate on the motives of collectors of such material — on the motives of buyers of such material too. Perhaps he would be grateful that such ephemeral (yet perennial) material had been preserved.

But this is going too far afield. *Colombo's Little Book* is meant to be a collection of humour for the literate layman, not the specialist scholar. It is meant to amuse and divert the reader. It is also something of a first. Although books of this sort have been successfully published in other countries, this is the first of its kind in Canada. I hope it will not be the last.

Innumerable people deserve to be thanked; let me acknowledge the help of a handful. Many of the items in this book were sent to me as the result of Don Bell's article on my ever-growing collection of quotations that appeared in *Weekend Magazine* during the summer of 1973. More recent items came to hand in the spring of 1975 when host Harry Brown and producer John Barbarash of "Metro Morning," a CBC Radio program heard in the Toronto area from seven-to-nine each weekday morning, invited listeners to submit their favourite examples of public humour. Winning entries were submitted by Lorna Hindle, Don Willmott, and Warner Winters and are published here. Both readers and listeners, then, had a hand in shaping this collection.

For unstinting effort in dreaming up other titles for this book I have to thank Doug Fetherling (who wanted to call it "Slightly Higher in Canada"), Cyril Greenland ("From See to Saw") and Martin Myers ("The Maple Leaf for Awhile"). Kudos go to Mel Hurtig for the present title. For fifteen years I have wanted to have a book of mine illustrated by Peter Whalley, of Morin Heights, Que., and now my wish has come true. Let me thank: Jan Walter, who edited the amorphous mass of manuscript; David Shaw who added illustrations and the proper typographical flourishes for which he is so respected; and Mel Hurtig (the compleat publisher and author's friend) who with his usual flair decided to add the book to his list.

Let me acknowledge, as well, the assistance of Stuart Ross and that of the librarians at the Metropolitan Toronto Central Reference Library, particularly the rare-book specialists in the Baldwin Room. Some of the proverbial lore came from antiquarian books, loaned by Asher Joram of Acadia Books in Toronto, and from *Canadian Folk-Lore* (1918), a collection of monographs that appeared in *The Journal of American Folk-*

Lore, Volume 31, Numbers 119-20. My wife Ruth, and our children, Theodore, Catherine and Jonathan, to whom the book is dedicated, all made contributions of their own.

I hope readers will do more than shake their heads, snap their fingers, clench their teeth, slap their thighs, stick out their tongues, or whatever it is that readers do when they encounter in books versions of bloopers and limericks that are inferior to the ones they know. I hope they will sit down, write out their superior versions, and send them to me at the address below. I covet them for future collections of light material, and will try to acknowledge all correspondence.

John Robert Colombo
42 Dell Park Avenue
Toronto, Ontario, Canada
M6B 2T6

Lore of the Land

"Proverbs are the wisdom of ages collected into a few brief words."

This definition of Susanna Moodie's dates back to 1852. No doubt she had in mind those proverbs and proverbial expressions that were current in Britain and common throughout the British colonies during the nineteenth century. It is doubtful that she was thinking of anything specifically Canadian.

Are there proverbs or proverbial expressions characteristic of Canada? Before one has a proverb, one has to have a people. Canada may be a country, but the Canadians are not a single people. We are a slew of people, so our "wisdom of ages" has not often taken root in a "few brief words." But we do have some distinctive ways of saying things, and some odd and unusual saws and sayings, as the following pages illustrate.

Three moves are as bad as a fire.

*

A going foot always gets something, if it is only a thorn.

*

The devil places a pillow for a drunken man to fall on.

*

Do not shout dinner till you have your knife in the loaf.

*

Twist my soul on the end of a fence rail.

*

May an Iroquois broil me.

*

If you're smart enough to be a farmer, you're too smart to be a farmer.

*

Three in a canoe beat two of a kind.

*

Half-pay officers never die.

*

Canada is a country with two official languages and no official culture.

*

Praise without profit puts little in the pocket.

*

Pity without relief is like mustard without beef.

*

My bark is on the sea, as the little dog said when he fell overboard.

*

All lawyers may be said to belong to the *Fee*-nian Brotherhood.

*

Scotch is the wine of the West.

*

May all your wrinkles come from happy smiles.

*

As Prince Albert goes, so goes the nation.

*

When our vices leave us, we flatter ourselves that we leave them.

*

By others' faults, wise men correct their own.

*

Money, like manure, does no good till it is spread.

*

What you lack in your head you make up in your heels.

*

When poverty comes in at the door, love flies out at the window.

*

Don't take a lazy man's load.

*

I won't buy a dog and do my own barking.

*

God knows but He won't tell.

*

If the Lord is willing and the Devil makes no objections. . . .

*

Speak of the Devil, and he is sure to appear.

*

Thanks killed the cat.

*

He's as slow as molasses in January.

*

I'll do it in two shakes of a dead lamb's tail.

*

May all your winds blow fair.

"Proverbs and Maxims are undoubtedly the most interesting and effectual media of imparting to the dawning mind the finest sentiments and the best moral precepts." So wrote George G. Vasey in his introduction to *The Classical English Spelling-Book* published in Montreal in 1862. Here are some of the proverbs and maxims he included in his primary-school reader.

Nothing can be polite
That is not good and right.

*

What can't be cured,
Must be endured.

*

The wheel that's weak
Is apt to creak.

*

Do not ride a free horse to death.

*

Our minds must be cultivated, as well as our plants.

*

If thou has Wit and Learning, get Wisdom and Modesty.

*

Study makes the eyes weak and the brains strong.

A Sampler of Wise and Witty Sayings
Compiled by Thomas Sellar of Montreal in 1866

The worst kind of oil to have anything to do with—turm oil.

*

The bottle is the Devil's crucible, in which everything is melted.

*

The difficulty of a fast man's life—chequing his tailor's bills.

*

A crusty old bachelor says women should be spelt whim-en.

*

What to expect at a hotel—inn-attention.

*

The ugliest hood in the world—falsehood.

*

The smaller the calibre of the mind, the greater the *bore* of a perpetually open mouth.

*

The oldest piece of furniture is the multiplication "table." It was constructed more than a thousand years ago, and it is as good as new.

*

At what time of life may a man be said to belong to the vegetable kingdom? When long experience has made him sage.

*

"My first I do; my second I do not; my whole you are." Love-ly [lie].

What about the native peoples of Canada? What is their proverbial lore like? Here are some colourful Eskimo proverbs and proverbial expressions:

Luck is better than long legs.

*

Trust the river but not the brook.

*

You do not know who is your friend or who is your enemy until the ice breaks.

Love comes after marriage.

*

A man's best friend is his dog, better even than his wife.

*

It is said that it is so, and therefore it is so.

Before you love, learn to run through the snow leaving no footprints.

*

May you have warmth in your igloo, oil in your lamp, and peace in your heart.

The Eskimos divide the year into thirteen periods of twenty-eight days each, according to the lunar cycle. Here is how their calendar runs, beginning with the January moon.

Kah-pid-rah	It is cold
Hir-ker-maun	The sun returns
Ik-ke-ar-par-roon	The sun is rising
A-von-eve	The baby seals are born
Neoh-e-a-ler-roon	The seals take to the water
Kav-ah-roc-vik	The time the seals shed their coats
Nook-rah-hah-le-yoon	The fawn of the caribou are born
Mun-cha-le-yoon	The birds are nesting
Ich-yah-yoon	The young birds are hatched
Ah-mer-ral-yoon	The caribou migrate
Noo-le-ah-le-yoon	The time to have a wife
See-koot-se-room	The ice is making in the bays
Sik-ker-ne-loon	The sun disappears

The source: *Archibald the Arctic* (1956), by Archibald Lang Fleming, the first bishop of the Arctic.

The Indians of Canada have proverbs and proverbial expressions too. Here are a few of them:

It is not enough for a man to know how to ride, he must know how to fall.

*

He who does not speak is not heard by God.

*

He who tells the truth doesn't sin, but he causes inconvenience.

*

A deer, although toothless, may accomplish something.

*

There is nothing so eloquent as a rattlesnake's tail.

*

He wants to die with all his teeth in his head.

*

May your horses always be swift, your buffalo instantly abound, and your women live long and always look young.

What follows is an instance of inadvertent humour from a grammar or primer of terms used by traders and trappers. "Chipewyan Conversation" originally appeared in *Voyages and Travels of an Indian Interpreter and Trader, Describing the Manners and Customs of the North American Indians* (1791), by J. Long.

I will go.
  Are you going, friend?
Yes, but I shall return soon.
  Have you any good guns?
Yes.
  Let us see them.
This is broke.
  This, I think, is a good one.
I want a paddle.
  Here is one for you.
Thank you, friend.
  Where is your wife?
She is dead.
  Is it long since?
Last winter.
  Have you any children alive?
Only one boy.
  Can he hunt?
Not yet.
  Where is your brother?
I saw him last winter at the Skunk's Lake.
  He was killed there by an Indian when he was drunk.

The oldest part of Canada is Newfoundland, which was the first of Britain's overseas colonies, so it is not surprising "the Great Island" has a wealth of proverbial lore, most of it concerned with the sea. Here are some proverbs known for centuries to Newfoundland fisherfolk:

He is as fine a man as ever broke a cake of the world's bread.

*

He is an honest man when there are no anchors around.

*

A fisherman is one rogue, a merchant is many.

*

Cape St. Mary's pays for all.

*

Empty vessels loom biggest.

*

Let no man steal your lines.

*

Pigs may fly, but they are very unlikely birds.

*

'Tis not every day that Morris kills a cow.

*

You are as deep as the grave.

*

Fair weather to you and snow to your heels.

Newfoundland place names are as inspired as Newfoundland folklore. Here are the names of some places that actually appear on the map:

Little Paradise
    Misery Point
Comfort Cove
    Confusion Bay
Heart's Delight
    Heartbreak Point
    *

Pigeon Island
    Gander Bay
Eagle Island
    Goose Bay
    *

Come-by-Chance
    Blow-me-Down
Run-by-Guess
    Bumble Bee Bight
Jerry's Nose
    Joe Blatt's Arm
Nancy Oh
    HaHa Bay
Bleak Joke Cove
    Little Hopping Harbour
    *

Bay D'Espoir
    Bay Despair
English Harbour
    Ireland's Eye
    *

Cow Head
    Dog Cove
Cat Gut
    Boat Point
Snake's Bight
    Fox Roost
Dragon Bay
    Lion's Den
    *

Shoe Cove
    Stocking Harbour
    *

Herring Neck
    Salmon Cove
Dog Fish Point
    Schooner Island
Boat Harbour
    Mooring Point
    *

False Cape
    Mistaken Point
    *
Cook's Harbour
    Spoon Cove
Bread Island
    Butter Cove
Mutton Bay
    Turnip Point
Sugar Loaf
    Cape Onion
Famine Point
    Famish Gut
    *

Triangle Point
    Round Harbour
Pyramid Point
    Square Islands
    *

Black Island
    White Bay
Red Island
    Orange Bay
Green Island
    Dark Cove
    *

Bareneed
    Empty Basket
Devil Cove
    God Bay
Harbour Grace
    Harbour Harbour

Proposed Names for Canada

The first European to use the word "Canada" was Jacques Cartier on his voyage of 1535. To the French explorer from St. Malo, it defined the region along the St. Lawrence River between present-day Quebec City and the future site of Montreal. Only in 1867 did Canada come to represent the Confederation of four British colonies in North America. There were some other suggestions for the name of that federal union, and here are a few.

Acadia
Albertoria
Albertsland
Albionora
Albona
Alexandrina
Aquilonia
Borealia
Britannia West
Britannica
British North America
Cabotia
Canadensia
Colonia
Efisga [a contraction of England, France, Ireland, Scotland, Germany, Aborigines]
Hochelaga
Laurentia
Mesopelagia
New Albion
Nicagarentia
Norland
Superior
Transatlantia
Transylvania
Tuponia [a contraction of The United Provinces of North America]
Ursulia
Vesperia
Victoralia
Victorialand
West Britannia

So many silly names were suggested that in the Confederation debates, on February 9, 1865, the patriot Thomas D'Arcy McGee stood up in the Legislative Assembly and made the following suggestion:

> One individual chooses Tuponia and another Hochelaga, as a suitable name for the new nationality. Now I would

ask any honourable member of this House how he would feel if he woke up some fine morning and found himself, instead of a Canadian, a Tuponian or Hochelagander. (Laughter.) I think, sir, we may safely leave for the present the discussion of the name as well as the origin of the new system . . . .

On the Road

This section is devoted to actual road signs that have been spotted by motorists and pedestrians on the highways and byways of Canada. These "signs of the times" tell us a lot about the people who make up this country, but what precisely I am not quite sure!

The sign that follows was erected by a stretch of muddy road between Swan Hills and Fort Assiniboine, Alta., in 1956:

   PICK YOUR RUT CAREFULLY
   You Will Be in It for the Next 80 Miles

Some prankster, driving along an Ontario secondary road near Lambeth in the 1940s, came across an attractive sign that read:

   LIVE IN LOVELY LAMBETH

He stopped, got out a can of paint and a brush, and altered a few letters. He drove away, leaving the sign to read:

   LOVE IN LIVELY LAMBETH

The following traffic warning is quite common throughout the country. This one was spotted in Charlottetown as early as 1950.

DRIVE SLOW AND SEE OUR CITY
DRIVE FAST AND SEE OUR JAIL

The road leading to the provincial jail, Lethbridge, Alta., runs off the main highway, where the following warning appears:

PROVINCIAL JAIL — KEEP OUT

Perhaps the most celebrated road sign in the country appeared, between 1963 and 1973, just outside the town of Biggar, west of Saskatoon. It read:

NEW YORK IS BIG
BUT THIS IS BIGGAR

Another amusing sign appeared on Highway 13, approaching Killam, Alta., about one hundred miles southeast of Edmonton:

> Drive Safely
> and Avoid Accidents
> KILLAM

And then there is this sign that advertises the wares of a small Saskatchewan town:

> TISDALE
> Land of Rape and Honey

Someone hastily erected his own road sign on Highway 9, on Saskatchewan soil, as he was entering Alberta, in 1971:

> THE LAST ONE OUT, TURN OUT THE LIGHT

A gentler note was sounded in the Maritimes, where outside Lawrencetown, N.S., this sign appeared:

LOVELY ELMS. DANGEROUS CURVES.

A sinister note is sounded by this road sign outside the village of Belle River, near Windsor, Ont.:

BELLE RIVER
Population 2,200
Radar Controlled

In Windsor itself, there is an intersection of two streets with amusing names:

SANDWICH ST. — CHEWIT ST.

A United Church minister, driving from Toronto to Peterborough in 1961, claims that he saw in farmers' fields a succession of billboards with the standard Biblical admonitions:

PREPARE TO MEET THY GOD!
JUDGEMENT DAY IS AT HAND!

Then he came upon a handpainted sign by the side of the road with the following existential maxim:

EXISTENCE PRECEDES ESSENCE

Existentialism may not be everyone's cup of tea, but speeding certainly is. At a service station on Highway 1, west of Hope, B.C., in 1972, a driver reported spotting this sign:

DRINK GIN AND HAVE THE RCMP FOR A CHASER

Popular even in Quebec (at Chateauguay, in 1972) is this billboard warning:

SMILE
You May be on Radar

The energy crisis of 1973 did not deter one Vancouver gas station operator from risking an atrocious pun:

FILL UP NOW AND BE TANKFUL

Black humour can be detected in this road sign advertisement for the Hawkswood Repair Service, Windsor, Ont.:

WE MEET BY ACCIDENT

And then there is the Vancouver street sign observed in 1973:

> To Cross Pacific
> Push Button and Wait
> For WALK Signal

One Ontario town welcomed visitors in the 1940s with:

> YOU ARE A STRANGER IN BROCKVILLE ONLY ONCE

The proud town of Bassano, Alta., boasts the Bassano Dam, the first irrigation dam built in Alberta and still in use. A sign at the town limits reads:

> BEST IN THE WEST BY A DAM SITE

Highway construction outside Nelson, B.C., was introduced in 1955 by:

> SORRY ABOUT THE NEXT 40 MILES
> (We Are Building You a Better Road!)

A sign posted at the Quebec-Ontario border in 1955 declared:

> FIRST CHANCE FOR MARGARINE!

This sign was spotted on a Quebec highway near Trois-Rivières by Lorna Hindle in 1969. With it she won the "Metro Morning" contest. It is very Canadian humour!

> HISTORIC SITE
> Under construction

A rancher from the B.C. interior posted this roughly painted sign on his gate in 1966:

> SURVIVING TRESPASSERS WILL BE PROSECUTED!

Finally, this notice which identifies the waterworks outside the village of Bath near Kingston, Ont.:

> BATH
> WATER
> FILTRATION
> PLANT

Lots of Limericks

That always witty and frequently bawdy five-line verse, the limerick, is said to owe its name to the city of Limerick, in the County of Limerick, in southern Ireland, where presumably the irreverent, poetry-loving Irish devised the devilishly difficult form.

There are Limericks in Canada — two, in fact. There is the Township of Limerick, in Hastings County, Ont., and the village of some three hundred souls, Limerick, Sask. Over the years the verse form has found favour in Canada. Yet it cannot be said to have flourished here, although from time to time it has flowered in these northern climes.

The limericks that are published here refer to place names that may be found on Canadian maps, although most of the names refer to places found on British maps. Many of the limericks are published here for the first time. All of them are amusing — and printable.

An Eskimo in Athabaska
Let his igloo to friends from Alaska.
    When they asked if his spouse
    Went along with the house,
He replied, "I don't know, but I'll aska."

There was a young girl from Chicoutimi
Who said, "This kind of date is quite new to me.
    I don't feel the same
    As I did when I came —
What on earth did you do to me?"

There was a young man of Eau Claire
Who had an affair with a bear.
    But the surly old brute
    With a snap of her snoot
Left him only one ball and some hair.

A strip-teaser up in Fall River
Caused a sensitive fellow to quiver.
    The esthetic vibration
    Brought a soulful elation.
Besides, it was good for his liver.

A reckless young man from Fort Blaney
Made love to a spinster named Janie.
    When his friends said, "Oh dear,
    She's so old and so queer,"
He replied, "But the day was *so* rainy!"

A Hamilton hi-fi Lothario
Wooed pretty young maids with his stereo.
    He turned it up loud
    As he proudly avowed,
"My pickup's the best in Ontario!"

Said a fair-headed maiden of Klondike,
"Of you I'm exceedingly fond, Ike.
    To prove I adore you
    I'll dye, darling, for you
And be a brunette, not a blonde, Ike."

A lady from near Lake Louise
Declared she was bothered by fleas.
    She used gasoline
    And later was seen
Sailing over the hills and the trees.

There was a young fellow of Leeds
Who swallowed a packet of seeds.
    In a month, silly ass,
    He was covered with grass
And he couldn't sit down for the weeds.

There was a young girl from Montreal
Who wore a newspaper dress to a ball
    But her dress caught on fire
    And burnt her entire
Front page — sporting section and all.

There was a young man from Montrose
Who could tickle himself with his toes.
    The trick was so neat,
    He fell in love with his feet,
And christened them Myrtle and Rose.

There was a young man of Moose Jaw
Who wanted to meet Bernard Shaw.
    When they questioned him, "Why?"
    He made no reply,
But sharpened an axe and a saw.

There was a young man from Perth,
Who was born on the day of his birth.
    He was wed, so they say,
    On his wife's wedding day,
And he died on his last day on earth.

A pregnant young miss of Placentia,
Who suffered from chronic dementia,
    Insisted her lapse
    Was caused by two chaps
Who raped her all night in absentia.

The I.O.D.E. in Port Hope
Are making an effort to cope
    With bearded, uncouth
    And undisciplined youth,
So they've switched from martinis to dope.

There was a young poet named Peck
Whose verse earned him many a cheque,
    Though he'd gathered them all
    From an old washroom wall
In the Government House in Quebec.

An important young man of Quebec
Had to welcome the Duchess of Teck;
    So he bought for a dollar
    A very high collar
To save himself washing his neck.

An eloquent young man named Damude
Said, "The family allowance is crude;
　　Every time a Quebecker
　　Whips out his old pecker,
Some taxpayer in Ontario gets screwed!"

There was a young girl from St. Cyr
Whose reflex reactions were queer.
　　Her escort said, "Mabel,
　　Get up off the table;
That money's to pay for the beer."

There was a young man from St. John's
Whose preference in girls was for blondes.
    But yet if he met
    A brunette who would pet,
He would date her without any qualms.

In the turbulent turgid St. Lawrence
Fell a luscious young damsel named Florence,
    Where poor famished fish
    Made this beautiful dish
An object of utter abhorrence.

A bright little maid in St. Thomas
Discovered a suit of pajhomas.
    Said the maiden, "Well, well!
    What they are I can't tell;
But I'm sure that these garments St. Mhomas."

Said a youth from Saskatchewan,
"You have something nobody can match you on.
    I'm referring, my dear,
    To a place at the rear,
That it gives me such pleasure to pat you on."

A boy at Sault Ste. Marie
Said, "Spelling is all Greek to me,
    Till they learn to spell 'Soo'
    Without any 'u',
Or an 'a' or an 'l' or a 't'!"

A heifer from up near the Soo
When approached by a bull answered, "Moo."
    Then she took the wrong track,
    And lay down on her back,
While the bull figured out what to do.

There was a young man of South Bay,
Making fireworks one summer day.
    He dropped his cigar
    In the gunpowder jar . . .
There *was* a young man of South Bay.

There was a young lady of Trent
Who said that she knew what it meant
    When he asked her to dine,
    Private room, lots of wine,
She knew, oh she knew — but she went!

The art-loving Bishop of Truro
Kept a nude by Renoir in his bureau.
    He said, "It's not smut
    That engrosses me but
Nineteenth-century chiaroscuro!"

There was an old maid of Vancouver,
Who captured a man by manoeuver.
    She jumped on his knee
    With some rare *eau de vie,*
And nothing on earth could remove her.

There was a dumb lady from York
Who at flesh-to-flesh contact would balk.
    "Don't you think that you are,"
    Said she, "going too far?
Why can't we just sit here and talk?"

A skinny old maid from Verdun
Wed a short-peckered son-of-a-gun.
    She said, "I don't care
    If there isn't much there.
God knows it is better than none."

A fruiterer, out of Wascana,
Grew the world's most expansive banana.
    He could normally swell
    Way beyond Fort Qu'Appelle
And, when specially roused, to Montana!

As the Scotchman once said to the Sphinx,
"I'd like just to know what he thinks,
    I'll ask him," he cried,
    And the Sphinx — he replied,
"It's the hell of a time between drinks."

A poet from Winnipeg, Man.,
Wrote verses that never would scan.
    When asked why this was,
    He replied, "Well, because
I always try to fit in as many words to a line as I can."

Not all limericks with "Canadian content" celebrate places. Some of them sing of the glories of former governor generals, of the country's native peoples, of the great universities across the land. . . .

As he lay in his bath, mused Lord Byng,
"Oh Vimy! What memories you bring!
    That gorgeous young trooper . . .
      No! No! Gladys Cooper!
By Gad, sir! That was a near thing."

There once was an elderly Cree
Who was mad about whisky in tea.
    He drank ninety-five cups,
    Gave a couple of brrups,
And died in his own warm tepee.

Ethnologists up with the Sioux
Wired home for two punts, one canoe.
    The answer next day
    Said, "Girls on the way,
But what the hell's a 'panoe'?"

One night a young amorous Sioux
Had a date with a maiden he knioux.
    The coroner found
    The couple had drowned
Making love in a leaky canioux.

There was a young student of Queen's
Who haunted the public latrines.
    He was heard in the john
    Saying, "Bring me a don —
But spare me those dreary old deans."

The best limericks are said to be the anonymous ones. But many very fine limericks were written by prominent people. Here are a few, beginning with "Relativity," the best-known limerick of all time.

There was a young lady named Bright
Whose speed was far faster than light;
    She set out one day
    In a relative way
And returned on the previous night.

The authorship of this limerick, which first appeared in *Punch*, December 19, 1923, was claimed by A. H. Reginald Buller, an authority on fungi who taught at the University of Manitoba. Buller's claim is acknowledged by William S. Baring-Gould in *The Lure of the Limerick* (1968), but is not enhanced by the fact that he is undoubtedly the author of the following sequel to "Relativity":

To her friends said the Bright one in chatter,
"I have learned something new about matter:
    My speed was so great,
    Much increased was my weight,
Yet I failed to become any fatter!"

Two limericks by British authors that are well-known in Canada are both about Quebec. The first, attributed to Rudyard Kipling, appeared in Stephen Leacock's *Humour and Humanity* (1937), and is a classic:

There was a young man of Quebec
Who was frozen in snow to his neck,
    When asked, "Are you Friz?"
    He replied, "Yes I is,
But we don't call this cold in Quebec."

The second is much older and comes from *The Book of Nonsense*, published in 1846 by Edward Lear:

There was an Old Man of Quebec,
A beetle ran over his neck;
    But he cried, "With a needle
    I'll slay you, O beadle!"
That angry Old Man of Quebec.

Perhaps the idea of writing a limerick about Quebec occurred to Lear after reading the nursery-rhyme limerick that appeared in R. S. Sharpe's *Anecdotes and Adventures of Fifteen Gentlemen* (1822):

> A tailor, who sailed from Quebec,
> In a storm ventured once upon deck;
> But the waves of the sea
> Were as strong as could be,
> And he tumbled in up to his neck.

The following limerick has its place in history and cannot be appreciated unless it is realized the limerick is about Gerda Munsinger, who admitted knowing at least one cabinet minister intimately, and was suspected of being a German spy. Gillis Purcell, former general manager of Canadian Press, won a *Maclean's Magazine* limerick contest in 1967 with the following tribute to Mrs. Munsinger:

> There was a young lady from Munich
> Whose bosom distended her tunic.
> Her main undertaking
> Was cabinet making
> In fashions *bilingue et unique*.

None other than Sir Gilbert Parker has the next limerick attributed to him. The Canadian-born historical novelist was a member of the British parliament from 1900 to 1918, and his limerick probably dates from that period.

> There was an old fellow of Croydon,
> Whose cook was a regular hoyden;
> She would sit on his knees
> When shelling the peas,
> Or similar duties employed on.

This one, on the town of Gimli, Man., appeared in Watson Kirkconnell's *Centennial Tales and Selected Poems* (1965):

There was a young lady of Gimli
Who sought to walk slender and slimly.
    She won her heart's wish
    On a diet of fish
And the gravedigger smiled rather grimly.

The following two limericks were written in idle moments by the archivist and historian, Norah Story:

There was a shy maiden of Guelph
Who would walk in the woods by herself;
    When required to tell
    Why she'd started to swell,
She replied that she'd talked to an elf.

There was a thin lady of Perth
Renowned far and wide for her mirth;
    Till one day in her glee
    She shouted, *"Oui! Oui!"*
And added eight pounds to her girth.

The writer David Helwig composed this witty limerick called "Paradise Lost":

There once was a God who said, "All
Men are predestined to fall
    (As Eve did when tempted)
    But will be redempted
With footnotes provided by Paul."

Anthologist and poet A. J. M. Smith is the author of the following:

A fat willing girl of Toronto
When asked, said, "Of course, if you want to,"
    And quickly reclined
    In a posture designed
To facilitate climbing up onto.

This verse was not composed by a writer but by an artist, and a Toronto artist at that, Mrs. Florence Vale Franck:

There was a young lady named Dinah
Who had an enormous vagina.
    If you gave a good shove
    Through the tunnel of love
You'd come out at Queen and Spadina.

And then there is the passel of limericks by Geoffrey B. Riddehough, a retired professor at the University of British Columbia, published in *Dance to the Anthill* (1972):

There was a young woman named Maud,
Whose coldness left every man awed,
    But they always would say,
    "We prefer her that way:
She's so dreadfully messy when thawed."

There was a young woman of Lillooet,
Who said, "I've so ugly a sillooet
    That I weep in my slumber
    And, times without number,
Wake up with one-half of my pillooet."

There is a young girl of Cape Ann,
Often seen in bed with a man:
    You see, they are weeding
    A bed where they're breeding
Chrysanthemums, yellow and tan.

There was a young Scot named McEwan,
Who was such an outrageous Don Juan
    That the whole parish met,
    Took him off to the vet,
And said, "Thot'll stop wit he's bin doing!"

There was a young woman of Brandon,
Who moved with the wildest abandon.
    The force of her weight
    (208)
Collapsed every lap she would land on.

There was a young poet of Bloor,
Who wrote limericks (often impure);
    But at last he eschewed
    Whatever was crude,
And his readers grew fewer and fewer.

Full Coarse Meals

Proprietors of restaurants in France are required by law to post their menus, complete with price lists, so passers-by can compare the fares and costs. Perhaps the same law should be passed in Canada. In any case, here are some unofficial signs, notes and details from the menus of Canadian eating establishments.

The earliest sign on record is the signboard outside the Half-Way House which opened for business in York (as Toronto was called in 1816):

> Within this hive we're all alive,
> Good liquor makes us funny;
> If you be dry step in and try
> The flavour of our honey.

If there is any doubt in the reader's mind about the nature of the "honey," it should be quickly dispelled by the sign that hung outside the Tecumseh Wigwam which flourished in the 1820s near Taddle Creek, Yorkville Village, now part of Toronto:

John Margetson, he lives here;
He sells brandy, wine and beer.

Here is a sign Stroller White, the Klondike newsman of local fame, recalled seeing outside a building opposite the Gold Belt Hotel, Dawson City, about 1901:

UNDERTAKING,
EMBALMING &
ICE CREAM PARLOR

There is no one to compare with the outspoken Joe Beef — the Irish-born proprietor of Joe Beef's Canteen at Common

and Callière, the hangout on the Montreal waterfront during the 1880s. Joe Beef made up terrific rhymes which he published on his menus and in his newspaper advertisements in prose form. Here are some of Joe's "beefs."

> Joe Beef of Montreal, the son of the People; he cares not for Pope, Priest, Parson or King William of the Boyne; all Joe wants is his Coin. He trusts in God in summer time to keep him from all harm; when he sees the frost and snow poor old Joe trusts in the Almighty Dollar and good old maple wood to keep his belly warm, for Churches, Chapels, Ranters, Preachers, Beechers, and such stuff Montreal has already got enough.

Some of Joe Beef's spirit survived the years. Sir Anthony Jenkinson dined at Ben's Cafe in Montreal fifty years later. The British traveller could not resist jotting down some of the verses that appeared there:

> Mary had a little lamb:
> What will you have?
>   *

Imported sturgeon
Needs no urgin'.

*

Use less sugar.
Stir like hell;
We don't mind the noise.

Frank Rasky, the journalist, likes to quote the wording of the sign in the lobby of the Stag Hotel in Porcupine, Ont.:

> We ain't the Waldorf-Astoria. If we were, you wouldn't be here. You ain't Pierpont Morgan. If you were, you wouldn't be here. We know this hotel is on the bum. What about yourself?

Then there is the following mouth-watering item from the menu of the Gaseteria Restaurant, Gananoque, Ont., in 1964:

> Jello du Jour ....15¢.

The sign that follows appeared in the beverage room of the Hotel Vancouver on Grey Cup Day, 1971:

NO SERVICE WILL BE PROVIDED AT THIS BAR
TO ANY CALGARIAN ON A HORSE

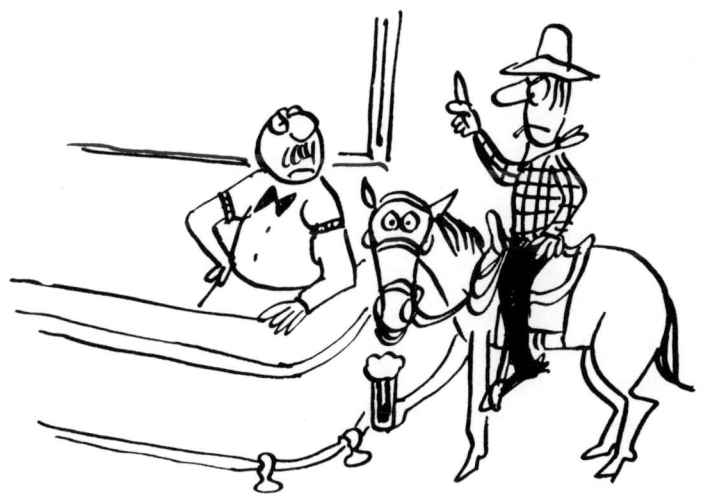

The following "daily special" has graced menus all across the West, from Manitoba to British Columbia:

    T-Bone   25¢.
    With Meat $4.00

The film critic Clyde Gilmour claims the following item actually appeared on the menu of a Winnipeg restaurant in 1952:

    Meat loaf *avec* green peas

The broadcaster Robert Zend observed the following notice in a Chinese restaurant in Bracebridge, Ont., in the early 1960s:

    The Wise Chinaman say:

    You ask for credit.
    I give.
    You no pay.
    I am mad.

    You ask for credit.
    I no give.
    You are mad.

    Better you are mad.

The poet Doug Fetherling recalls with a chuckle this boast which appears on the menu of a "greasy spoon" at the intersection of Bathurst and Dupont streets in Toronto:

    VESTA LUNCH — Reputable Since 1955

And from the menu of The Noshery, a Toronto restaurant specializing in Jewish cuisine:

    The Reuben

    The American Sandwich Sensation
    It's Inter-married!

> Corned Beef with Virginia Ham
> with Swiss Cheese with Cole Slaw
> all grilled together on Double Rye
> with French Fries

This item appeared on a menu at a greasy spoon, Pincher Creek, Alta., 1970:

> Creamed Aspirin Tablets
> on Toast
> with Coffee
>
> 50¢.

One problem shared by numerous restaurateurs in eastern Canada seems to be bad spelling. Signs have appeared in restaurants from Roddickton, Nfld., to Wingham, Ont., that have proudly boasted:

FULL COARSE MEALS

Let us hope the proprietors of these establishments do not cook as poorly as they spell.

The Other Place

Johns

At some point we have to approach the subject of lavatory humour, or jottings on the johns across the nation. Since we have noted the anonymous humour associated with food and drink, it is appropriate to turn our thoughts to more private matters — before directing our attention to loftier and more inspiring subjects. The items that follow have graced Canadian washroom walls, or disgraced them!

On a primitive privy at Baddeck, Cape Breton, N.S., appeared this piece of doggerel in the 1920s:

> No use to stand upon the seat,
> Bras d'Or crabs jump twenty feet.

A social scientist, with pen and paper in hand, noted this addition to the wall of a men's room in Alberta in 1928:

> When adam was a
> small lad before
> paper was invented
> he wiped his ass on
> a tuft of grass & went
> away contented

The following inscription, observed in the men's room at the restaurant in the international airport at Gander, Nfld., during the 1950s, is commonplace enough to be ranked as a cliché or a classic, depending on how many times one has heard or seen it:

> We aim to please.
> You aim too, please.

From the same decade comes the following, from a Nova Scotian privy:

> WHY GO WEST WHEN YOU CAN MAKE YOUR PILE HERE?

Scrawled on the wall above the urinals in the CPR Hotel in London, Ont., in 1960, appeared this gem:

> YOU DON'T BUY YOUR BEER HERE —
> YOU JUST RENT IT

Informants tell me the above wording has appeared in toilets across the country. Perhaps unique — but then again perhaps not — are the notices that appeared on the doors of the women's and men's washrooms at the Blairmore Golf Club in Alberta in 1960:

> SETTERS   POINTERS

Quite common, in men's johns, are variations on this admonition:

> Pilots with short engine mounts —
> Please taxi up close

Reporters on the *Sault Ste. Marie Star* claim that their irrepressible editor during the 1940s, Jim Curran, had this sign erected above the men's urinal:

> SHORTHORNS STAND CLOSE.
> THE MAN BEHIND YOU MAY BE IN HIS BARE FEET.

A sign over a W.C. in a tourist home in Barrie, Ont., in 1966, warned:

> DON'T PUT ANYTHING ELSE DOWN THIS TOILET

Not uncommon is the admonition:

> PLEASE DO NOT THROW CIGARETTE BUTTS INTO URINAL

To this notice — above the men's urinal at the Toronto Bus Depot during the 1960s — someone added:

> IT MAKES THEM SOGGY AND HARD TO LIGHT

Farley Mowat recalls this notice:

> LATRINES: All troops will ensure that faces are covered with soil after each person has deprecated.

It was an official order to the Hastings and Prince Edward Regiment, Northern Italy, spring, 1944. Farley Mowat in *The Regiment* (1955) called this "a most remarkable entry in the stilted argot of staff language. Some typist had not been equal to the need."

The energy crisis of 1972 took on new significance when someone scribbled the following message above a toilet in a camping ground in Nova Scotia:

> THE U.S. WANTS OUR WATER — FLUSH TWICE

The final example of washroom humour is a rebus — a word composed not of letters but of figures. This rebus appeared as a sign on the washroom door of a restaurant on the Trans-Canada Highway between Grand Falls and Cornerbrook, Nfld., in 1972:

4U2P

Churches

Although the churches in Canada are not run by people noted for their humour, the wit of the following signs and notices is often of the quite advertent variety.

Perhaps the most talked-about church sign in the country appears in front of St. James Anglican Church on busy Highway 4 at Neepawa, Man. It reads, to the delight of motorists and pedestrians:

> DRIVE CAREFULLY.
> YOU MIGHT HIT
> AN ANGLICAN.

The following welcoming message appeared on the lawn of St. Jude's Church, London, Ont.:

> COME IN AND HAVE YOUR FAITH LIFTED

Outside a Protestant church at Wasaga Beach, Ont., at the entrance to the parking lot, stands this sign:

> ANGEL PARKING ONLY

On the grounds of a church just south of Almonte, Ont., may be read this encouraging message:

> SIN NOW — PAY LATER

When a suburban church was all but demolished by the tornado that hit Sudbury in 1970, this sign was erected amid the rubble:

> PRAISE THE LORD, ANYWAY!

Posted outside a church in Toronto, 1969:

> WORK FOR THE LORD
> The pay isn't much
> But the retirement benefits
> Are out of this world

These signs have been preserved (if not observed) by the joke-collector Al Boliska:

> CHURCH PROPERTY
> Dumpeth Not
>
> *
>
> CLOSED
> For Re-prayers
>
> *
>
> COME UNTO GOD
> Use Next Door
>
> *
>
> KEEP OFF!
> This Means Thou

And, finally, the following message appeared on a signboard outside Riverside Church in Toronto in 1973:

> TIME TO ACT.
> JESUS IS COMING.
> Call Jimmy
> 368-4868

Laughing Matters

No book of Canadian humour would be complete without a couple of Newfie jokes. Now, you will not find an entry for "Newfie joke" in any dictionary. No one seems to remember when Newfoundlanders began telling jokes against each other, but it was about 1968 that they were first heard on the mainland. Wherever Canadians congregate, especially in St. John's, Nfld., someone is certain to begin by saying, "Did you hear the one about the Newfie who . . . ?"

A Newfie phoned Air Canada and asked the girl how long it took for a jet to go from Newfoundland to Toronto. The girl, being very busy at the time, replied, "One second, sir."
The Newfie replied, "Thank you."
*

Newfie: Do you like tongues?

Nova Scotian: I can't eat anything that comes from an animal's mouth.

Newfie: Would you like some eggs instead?

*

Torontonian: Come on, Newfie, tell me a joke.

Newfie: Why tell it, I'm looking at it.

*

Question: What is black and blue, and floats in the bay?

Answer: A mainlander who tells Newfie jokes.

The experienced Newfie joke collector is Bob Tulk, of Mount Pearl, Nfld., who has published a raft of booklets of such provincial lore. Tulk introduces each of his publications with the following author's note: "This book was published, not for the purpose of making fun of Newfoundlanders, but to show that most of us can take a joke as well as give one." The three jokes told here come from Tulk's first collection. His books are *Newfie Jokes* (1971), *New Newfie Jokes* (1972), *Bob Tulk's Newfie Jokes* (1973), *Even Funnier Newfie Jokes* (1974), with (no doubt) many more to follow!

And then there is the story of the psychiatrist who tried a word-association test on his sex-obsessed patient.

"What do you think of when I say 'chair'?"
"Sex."
"When I say 'dog'?"
"Sex."
"When I say 'tractor'?"
"Sex."
"Vagina?"
"Saskatchewan."

When the U.S.S.R. made its first wheat purchase from Canada in 1964, the following joke circulated in the Soviet Union, according to John Kolasky in *Look Comrade — The People are Laughing* (1972).

"Why were we able to buy wheat from Canada?"
"Due to a shortcoming of capitalism — overproduction."

A John Bull, conversing with an Indian, asked him if he knew that the sun never sets on the Queen's dominions.

"No," said the Indian.

"Do you know the reason why?" asked John.

"Because God is afraid to trust an Englishman in the dark," was the native's reply.

Howlers

What follow are howlers, or statements that were meant to be taken straight but can only be read obliquely. They come from second-year compositions submitted to O. J. Stevenson who from 1916 to 1939 headed the English Department at the Ontario Agricultural College in Guelph.

Around the house there should be shrubs and flowers with a good perennial boarder.

*

No sound was heard except the rattle of dishes broken occasionally by someone asking for a second helping.

*

To be a good driver a person should never lose his head and obey all traffic regulations.

*

One of the advantages of the automobile is that people who have cars of their own can go to their destiny whenever they like.

*

Everyone seemed happy and contented as they rushed to and fro from place to place.

From a York University Sociology Examination

The reason I have resorted to writting in pencil is so as I can correct some of my many spelling errors. Bare with me.

*

Women who go to work are masculated.

*

Ideally, universities should be set in a free environment in order that students, with the aid of faculty, may pursue their own interest in abstaining an education.

*

Compared to men, women have more faucets of emotion.

*

Twenty years ago, there were a limited number of Canadian municipalities that had a professional staff on the fingers of one hand.

*

In Cantonville, Quebec, the white people still buy their goods from French-speaking owned and operated stores.

From Grade XIII examinations, Ontario, 1950s and 1960s

During the banquet Macbeth goes out into the hall and has a soliloquy.

*

By the end of the play Macbeth is isolated from everybody except the reader.

*

A martyr is a person who dies solely for the thing he believes in when there is no other alternative.

*

The glory of becoming a martyr is certainly a grave temptation.

*

When Lear says, "Off, unbutton here," he is showing the essence of a man.

*

Rich [in Bolt's *A Man for All Seasons*] has no principles. He thinks nothing of cutting More's throat behind his back.

*

Santiago [in Hemingway's *The Old Man and the Sea*] is old and also holds a responsible position, he is captain and crew of his own skiff.

*

The sea to him is a precious lady who either grants or holds back gifts from the men who ride her.

*

[George] Orwell states what wonderful creatures these coal miners are sweating to the bone in their shifts down the shaft.

*

The simile is good in the first line because you read it then you wonder — what the hell is he talking about?

*

The simile is effective through the use of the word "skein" which conjures up all sorts of images in one's mind, especially if the word is not in one's vocabulary.

*

She seems unable to find anything interesting either in the flora or the filthy fauna of the poor.

*

Q. What is the importance of Sentence 7 in the paragraph?

A. Sentence 7 is of great numerical importance in the paragraph. Without it, Sentence 6 would be followed by Sentence 8.

These students' howlers were saved from oblivion by Warner Winters who won a "Metro Morning" prize with them.

The following sentences are said to be taken from letters

received by the Welfare Department of the Ministry of National Health and Welfare during the 1960s:

I am forwarding my marriage certificate and my six children. I had seven but one died which was baptized on a half sheet of paper.

*

I am writing to say that my baby was born two years old. When do I get my money?

*

Mrs. Jones has not had any clothing for a year and has been visited by the clergy regularly.

*

I am glad to report that my husband who was reported missing is now dead.

*

This is my eighth child. What are you going to do about it?

*

Please find for certain if my husband is dead. The man I live with now cannot eat or do anything till he knows.

*

I am very much annoyed to find that you have branded my boy an illiterate, as this is a dirty lie. I was married to his father a week before he was born.

*

I am forwarding my marriage certificate and my three children, one of which was a mistake as you will see.

*

In answer to your letter, I have given birth to a boy weighing 10 lbs. I hope this is satisfactory.

*

My husband got his cut off two weeks ago and I haven't had any relief since. Unless I get my husband's money pretty soon I will be forced to live an immortal life.

*

You have changed my boy to a girl. Will this make any difference?

*

Please send money at once. I have fallen in error with my landlord.

*

I have no children as my husband is a bus driver and works day and night.

*

In accordance with instructions I have given birth to twins in the enclosed envelope.

*

I want money quick as I can get it. I have been in bed with the doctor two weeks and he doesn't do me any good. If things don't improve I will have to send for another doctor.

Bloopers

Speaking of artificial insemination of cattle, it's a real male order business.

Farm reporter on CBC Radio from Vancouver during the 1950s.

Bill Mahoney's a marvellous breast stroker!

Irene Macdonald, former Olympic diver, praising the winner of the men's swimming event on CBC-TV during the 1960s.

Don't put words in my mouth — it's unsanitary.

Joe Pyne on "Speak Your Mind" on a private radio station, Montreal, 1961.

As I was saying, a fellow's lucky to get his seed back these days.

Peter Whittall — the future Mr. Fixit — commenting over CBC Radio during the 1930s on the birth of a four-pound, seven-ounce daughter during a period of extreme drought.

Kid's Bloopers

I'm a blunderful boy!

*

Don't worry, I'll stay calm, cool and collective!

*

"Cheeze-Whiz loves me, this I know . . ."

*

Snow is when clouds come down in little pieces — that's snow.

*

Jack Spratt could eat no fat,
  His wife could eat no lean;
And so betwixt them both, you see,
  Vicks and Vaseline!

*

A fag is a guy who goes around kissing girls.

*

Hey, mom, it's freezing hot outside!

*

Look, genuine stones!

> Dear Sirs:
>   I am told the T. Eaton Co. can furnish any thing asked for. Now I lost my wife over a year ago and I am very lonely living alone. Can you send me a woman not too old? I own my own house here. I have $67 a month income.

Letter sent by a Hamilton gentleman in 1952 to Eaton's Catalogue.

The following definition of "eunuch" appeared in *Highroad's Dictionary*, which was used during the 1940s in Canadian primary schools:

EUNUCH. A king's chamberlain.

Here is an unintended pun. It comes from "Memorandum for the Information of Applicants for Engagement in the North-West Mounted Police" of 1874:

Married men will not be engaged.

What follow are some verbal curiosities of Canadian interest. A *palindrome* is a word or phrase that reads the same forwards and backwards. A word like "noon" is a simple palindrome. Here are more complicated ones:

No sot nor Ottawa law at Toronto, son!

*

No Dot nor Ottawa "legal age" law at Toronto, Don.

*

Niagara, O roar again!

An *anagram* is a word or phrase composed of the letters of another word or phrase. "File" is a simple anagram of "life". Here are the names of two provinces, plus the anagram they yield.

Nova Scotia and Prince Edward Island.
Two Canadian Provinces: Lands I dread!

An *acrostic* is a message made up of the initial letters of words or lines of verse. No doubt accidentally, it came about that the names of four adjacent Montreal streets spell out the name of a minority that once made the area its home:

J ean Mance St.
E splanade St.
W averley St.
S t. Urbain St.

A *malapropism* — usually shortened to plain malaprop — is a remark that is unintentionally amusing because it mixes metaphors or misuses a single word. The late Sam Goldwin was a master of the malaprop. Many Canadians have contributed to malapropery; in fact, malaprops might be considered a characteristic form of Canadian expression.

Chief Dave Courchene of Manitoba got carried away in an interview on CBC-TV in 1973. "We're not fooling around," he explained heatedly. "We've got the bull by the tail, and we're looking him straight in the eye."

Torontonians are still chuckling over the malaprops minted by Allan Lamport. The former mayor once said: "If somebody's gonna stab me in the back, I wanna be there." On another occasion he was quoted as saying, "Why, I even went so far as to be fair." This last "Lampy" is a favourite of many: "Let's not just discontinue it, let's stop it!"

There is some question as to whether Slaw Rebchuck's malaprops are calculated or not. The Winnipeg councillor claims they are; his fellow councilmen claim they trip effortlessly from his lips. Here are a few anyway. Rebchuck once told a council meeting: "We're in total darkness but I see the light." To a city clerk who was presenting a lengthy report, he snapped: "Just give me the headlights." And on another occasion he was overheard saying, "They're making a mountain out of a molehole."

Another master of the malaprop is John Kushner, a former Calgary alderman, who has delighted the city council with such remarks as: "I'm not talking about businessmen, I'm talking about people." That was made in 1970. The following year he offered a suggestion: "Let's get face to face and face reality." "I want to hear from the expertise," he explained at a conference. On another occasion he informed everyone: "Remember, there's only one taxpayer — you and me." Another time he said: "Well, don't get your dandruff up." Finally, there is Kushner's classic remark: "I'm not sure very many of us can understand all this legal jargle."

When he was leader of the Social Credit Party, the Alberta businessman Robert Thompson uttered some beauties. Thompson's malaprops are nationally known. "You've buttered your bread," he once said, "now you have to lie in it." "If this thing starts to snowball, it will catch fire right across the country," Thompson declared at one meeting. When the British pound collapsed, the Social Creditor was heard to say, "I hope this is not going to be another financial crisis." This widely quoted remark is his finest: "The Americans are our best friends, whether we like it or not."

Phillip A. Gaglardi has numerous nicknames like "Dusty Rhodes" and "Flying Phil," which are allusions to the fast driving of the former minister of public works in the British Columbia Social Credit government. "I wasn't driving too fast, I was flying too low," he explained to a police officer who stopped him for speeding. "The only time I tell a lie is when I think I am telling the truth," he once declared. A lesser-known Gaglardi-ism is classic: "People shouldn't get excited about reports of pollution of the oceans. Everybody knows that oil and water don't mix."

Finally there is the inimitable Edith Josie, Indian correspondent for *The Whitehorse Star*, who resides in Old Crow, six hundred miles north of Whitehorse. Her reports on the state of things in the little settlement invariably begin: "Here are the news." No matter how difficult things are, Edith Josie will say "Everything good now." And her report will end: "This is end the news."

Conundrums from the 1860s

Why is a lady who flirts with every man she meets like a person whose skin cracks in cold weather? (Because she is liable to have chaps on her hands.)

*

Why is a philosopher like a looking-glass? (Because he reflects.)

*

Why is true wit like a diamond? (Because it cuts as well as it shines.)

*

Why is hunting for honey like a legacy? (Because it is a *bee*-quest.)

*

Why are miners like nervous people? (Because they are *ore* [o'er] anxious.)

*

Why is a fool like twenty hundred weight? (Because he's a simple-ton.)

*

Why is England like Japan? (Because it worships yellow sovereigns.)

*

Why is the letter "t" like an island? (Because it is in the midst of "water.")

*

Why is the letter "t" like your nose? (Because it goes before you [u].)

*

Why may carpenters reasonably believe there is no such thing as stone? (Because they never *saw* it.)

*

Why is it unlikely that an omnibus will be struck by lightning? (Because it always has a conductor.)

*

Why is the author the most peculiar of animals? (Because his tale comes out of his head.)

*

Why is a bridegroom at the altar like a sailor? (Because he's a marr'in her.)

*

Why is electricity like the police when they are wanted? (Because it's an invisible force.)

*

Why are cobblers eligible for medical diplomas? (Because they are all skilled in the art of heeling.)

*

Why are young ladies' affections always doubtful? (Because they are only Miss-givings.)

*

When is a cigar like an old maid? (When there is no match for it.)

*

When is a ship like a nobleman's wife? (When she's fastened to a pier.)

*

When is a boat like a heap of snow? (When it's a-drift.)

*

What musical instrument has had an honorary degree conferred upon it? (Fiddle, D.D.)

*

What is the greatest stand ever made for civilization? (The ink-stand.)

The preceding conundrums were collected by Thomas Sellar, a Montreal journalist and publisher, who issued them, along with lots of advertising matter, in a slim booklet called *"Choice Fragments": Being a Collection of Wise and Witty Sayings* (1866).

Four Tongue Twisters

Three gray geese and three green ganders; gray were the geese, and green were the ganders.

*

She sawed sick, slick, sleek, slim, slender saplings.

*

A big black bug bit a big black bear.

*

The sun shines on the shop signs.

Signs and Headlines

REHABILITATE SPEED FREAKS

Placard waved in front of "Flying Phil" Gaglardi, Nelson, B.C., 1970, when the Social Credit minister with a notorious speeding record was coming down hard on drug users.

WE LOVE OUR CHILDREN — DON'T LET PHIL DRIVE

Placard, Kimberly, B.C., 1972; a reference to the same Social Credit cabinet minister.

THE NEW DIMENSIONS OF MODERN ENVIRONMENTAL SANITATION

Sign on a dump truck, Toronto, 1963.

WELCOME LIBERACE AND OUR PRIME MINISTER

Sign outside a Holiday Inn in an Ontario city, 1963, noted by Lester B. Pearson in his memoirs.

SHAKESPEARE NON, MOLIÈRE OUI

Sign waved by schoolchildren during a protest against English-language instruction in Quebec schools, 1963.

BREST OR BUST

Sign painted on a Canadian Army jeep on the road to Brest, France, noted by World War II correspondent Wallace Reyburn.

HUSTLE GRAIN, NOT WOMEN

Placards carried by feminists at a gathering attended by Pierre Elliott Trudeau in Vancouver, August 8, 1969.

THANK BUDDHA IT'S TUESDAY

Poster on the wall of a Winnipeg radio station, November 1974.

THE REAL REVOLUTIONARIES
ARE THE RICH
WHO ARE WILLING TO ACT FOR JUSTICE

Sign outside a downtown Vancouver church, observed by Allan Fotheringham in 1970.

IT'S UNAMERICAN TO BE CANADIAN

Slogan on a poster produced by the Committee for an Independent Canada, 1972.

I LIKE THE JOB
IT'S THE WORK I HATE

Sign seen at Payne's Meat Market, St. Catharines, Ont., 1972.

MANY A LOVE NEST
IS UPSET BY A LARK

On a church bulletin-board, Aurora, Ont., 1970s.

SATISFACTION GUARANTEED OR YOUR HONEY BACK

Sign on a divorce lawyer's wall, Hamilton, Ont., 1975.

HISTORIC PLAQUE

Upon this stone on August 2nd, 1789, sat Alexander Mackenzie whilst fighting mosquitoes and planning his present (Imperial Oil Company) refinery. Since that date this stone has been a saluting point for dogs, foxes, and wolves, in honour of the man who led the missionaries, fur traders, tuberculosis and tin cans down this great river to the Polar Sea.

Lacking matches, cigarettes, radio, Esso gasoline, rubber boots and tissue paper, Mackenzie made the round

> trip from Lake Athabaska to the Frozen Ocean in 102 days, in a bark canoe powered by internal combustion Indians. Modern pioneers complain if the toast is cold or the mail plane is late.
>
> This plaque erected by the Bureau of Sights and Sites. Contractors; Sherwood & Associates. History made and/or Repaired.

According to the late Blair Fraser this plaque was erected in the 1950s by Angus Sherwood, the postmaster of Norman Wells, N.W.T., on a boulder outside his house on the bank of the Mackenzie River.

Headlines

> Another Blow for Unlucky Family
> Ted Kennedy Survives Crash

The Ottawa Journal, June 20, 1964.

> Thirty-four percent of all adolescents agree that having sex together is a good way for two people to become acquainted.

The Montreal Star, February 20, 1973.

> There is room in Williams Lake for an honest lawyer.

This line appeared in a weekly newspaper published in Williams Lake during the 1940s. "The town's *only* lawyer sued for libel," recalled former B.C. Chief Justice J. O. Wilson. "He was awarded damages of $1.00."

> Canadians Selling Deodorant
> Witness Revolution in Lisbon

The Toronto Star, April 29, 1974.

Man Saved from Ottawa
The Ottawa Journal, September 7, 1973.

Christmas Day Still December 25.
The Ottawa Citizen, November 24, 1972.

Museum Officials Stand Behind Nudes
A headline in a Victoria newspaper concerning an aesthetic problem.

School Board Bans Sex Behind Closed Doors
A headline in a Toronto paper in 1949 concerning sexual references in textbooks. This was inevitably followed by: "Board approves sex in very modified form."

"The Most Sensational Newspaper Headlines Imaginable"
 (As imagined by readers of *Maclean's,* February, 1967)

Pope Weds Pill Heiress
 *
Fathers of Confederation All Bachelors; Canada Proved Illegitimate
 *
Lunar Landing Craft Returns; Moon Mere Optical Illusion
 *
Doctors Say Cigarettes Only Cure for Common Cold
 *
Canadian Identity Found; Hundreds of Commentators Jobless
 *
Quebec's H-Bomb No Threat to Other Provinces, Says Daniel Johnson
 *
Dionne Quints A Hoax; 5 Couples Charged in Conspiracy

Officious Notices

When the first Parliament Building in Ottawa was destroyed in the disastrous fire of 1916, the government had to meet in emergency quarters. Suitable accommodation was found in the Royal Victoria Museum. The Senate, it was noted at the time, met in a gallery with the following words on the door:

PREHISTORIC FOSSILS

The official (and often officious) nature of bilingualism in this country has been commented on from time to time. A British journalist, travelling in Quebec in 1921, noted the following warning near power cables in Joliette, which he explained was written "in French, English, and American":

PAS D'ADMISSION
NO ADMISSION
KEEP OUT

Prisoners at St. Vincent de Paul Penitentiary in Montreal must have smiled when their new library opened in 1935. The shelf for serious magazines like *The Canadian Forum* and *The New Yorker* was marked:

FOR THE USE OF ILLITERATES ONLY

The following request was observed in Banff National Park in 1971:

TAKE ONLY PICTURES
LEAVE ONLY FOOTPRINTS

Eleven years earlier, visitors to the same Alberta park were amused when they spotted a new, hastily erected sign beside the regular sign, which was an arrow pointing to Mt. Eisenhower that read:

MT. EISENHOWER, alt. 8750′

Beside it someone erected his own sign, which pointed down and said:

MT. KHRUSCHEV, alt. 4′6″

This was during the Soviet premier's dramatic attendance at the summit conference in Paris, May 16, 1960. The sign was quickly and quietly removed by the park warden.

Toronto subway passengers always consider themselves suitably warned when they read this bold warning at the Davisville subway stop:

CAUTION
Trespassers May Be Electrocuted

Near the federal prison at Cowansville, Que., somebody erected his own sign on a convenient telephone pole, following a series of prison breaks in the early 1960s:

WATCH FOR PRISONERS CROSSING

Perhaps it was an ecologist who encouraged the city fathers of Creston, B.C., to put up this anti-pollution sign:

OBEY YOUR SENSE OF SMELL —
THAT'S AN ODOUR!

But the most mysterious of all signs is a government warning. It appears at the entrance to the Christian Island Indian Reserve, Georgian Bay, Ont., and it reads:

YOU ARE NOW ENTERING
AN INDIAN RESERVATION
Please Act Accordingly

And then there are the following signs, all of which have adorned Canadian walls over the years.

ALL TALK ABOUT EUROPEAN POLITICS FORBIDDEN
By Order, R.C.M.P.

This admonition appeared in a beer parlour in Timmins, Ont., 1940.

NO SWEARING PLEASE.
THERE MAY BE GENTLEMEN PRESENT.

This sign greeted workers at a shipyard at Halifax, N.S., 1942.

WHAT DO YOU EXPECT OF A DAY
THAT STARTS BY GETTING OUT OF BED?

Handwritten sign on a students' bulletin board, Royal Military College, Kingston, Ont., 1970.

IF NOTHING ELSE WORKS —
PLEASE FOLLOW INSTRUCTIONS

Request on the employee's notice board at a Toronto manufacturing firm, 1971.

KWITCHERBITCHIN

Name on a rural cottage, Bromont Ski Area, Eastern Townships, Que., 1950.

THIS IS GOD'S COUNTRY.
DON'T SET FIRE TO IT
AND MAKE IT LOOK LIKE HELL.

Warning in the lobby of the Mountainview Hotel, Rocky Mountain House, Alta., 1950.

DANCE
EVERY SATURDAY NIGHT
THIS WEEK

Advertising marquee for a night club on the eastern shore of Nova Scotia, 1970.

THIS ELEVATOR DOES NOT RISE ON ASCENSION DAY

Sign on an elevator in Montreal in the 1930s. This notice was the basis of a well-known poetic satire by F. R. Scott.

DOGS SHALL NOT ENTER THESE PREMISES

Elaborate sign in the window of a Montreal florist's shop in Westmount, Que., 1973.

NOTICE

Executives who do not have secretaries of their own may take advantage of the girls in the stenographic pool.

Allegedly posted on a bulletin board at the CBC in Toronto, 1965.

DARK ROOM
IF YOU OPEN THE DOOR
ALL THE DARK WILL LEAK OUT

Sign on the dark room door in the photographic department of Sheraton College, Toronto, 1975.

PEOPLE WHO READ SIGNS
SHOULD HAVE THEIR EYES CHECKED

Advertisement for an optometrist's shop, Ottawa, 1975.

NOTICE

Our medical department recently received a complaint from Dr. Freedman that he has received numerous calls from CP employees regarding annual medical examinations. Please be advised that Dr. N. B. Freedman passed away last August, and you should not try to contact his office for examinations.

Superintendent's notice on the bulletin board at the head office of Canadian Pacific Railway, Montreal, 1973.

Rhymes & Reasons

"Let me make the songs of a nation," wrote Andrew Fletcher in 1703, "and I care not who makes its laws." No one really knows who first wrote or sang the verses and rhymes in this section, so the editor is as free to reproduce them as the reader is free to enjoy them. Some of these ditties make a lot of sense; others make . . . well . . . nonsense, which is a kind of sense too!

> Hail our great Queen in her regalia;
> One foot in Canada, the other in Australia.

This couplet has been attributed to "a Nova Scotian bard" and was supposedly composed "at the turn of the century."

> Rabbits hot and rabbits cold,
> Rabbits young and rabbits old,
> Rabbits tender and rabbits tough,
> Thank the Lord, I've had enough.

This ditty dates from the 1880s, and was recited by settlers on the prairies who lived off the land.

> How are your potatoes?
> Very small.
> How do you eat them?
> Skins and all!

The Canadian-born British press lord, Lord Beaverbrook, quoted this ditty in the 1930s and identified it as "a New Brunswick folk song."

> Dearly beloved brethren, is it not a sin,
> That when we eat potatoes, we throw away the skin?
> The skin feeds the pigs, and the pigs feed you,
> Dearly beloved brethren, is it not tuh-roo?

Doggerel quoted by Selwyn Dewdney in his novel *Wind without Rain* (1946).

> I'm English Bill,
> Never worked, an' never will.
> Get away girls,
> Or I'll tousle your curls.

Ditty sung by Billy Barker, who discovered gold in the Cariboo in 1862 and lent his name to Barkerville, B.C.

> Barr, Barr, wily old Barr,
> He'll do you all's much as he can;
> You bet he will collar
> Your very last dollar
> In the valley of the Saskatchewan.

This piece of doggerel — about the Reverend Isaac Barr, who led British colonists to settle the Lloydminster, Sask., area in 1903 — was recited during the following decade. The imperialist once told a reporter he had come "to claim Canada for the bleedin' Hempire."

> Some men love honour,
> Other men love groats,
> Here Wolfe reaped laurels,
> Lord Dalhousie, oats.

Ditty about Lord Dalhousie, governor in chief of Canada from 1819 to 1828, who is said to have sown and raised a crop of oats on the Plains of Abraham where General James Wolfe died in 1759. Quoted by Robina and Kathleen Macfarlane Lizars in *In The Days of the Canada Company* (1896).

> Come hither, come hither, my little dog Ponto,
> Let's trot down and see where Little York's gone to;
> For forty big Tories, assembled in junta,
> Have murdered poor Little York in the City of Toronto.

Doggerel attributed to William Lyon Mackenzie, first mayor of Toronto when the town of York was incorporated as the city of Toronto, March 6, 1834. Quoted by Robina and Kathleen Macfarlane Lizars in *Humours of '37: Grave, Gay and Grim* (1897).

> Oh, much I wish that I was able
> To build a house like Cartwright's stable,
> For it does cause me great remorse
> To be worse lodged than Cartwright's horse!

Verse written by Dr. James Sampson, mayor of Kingston, on Rockwood, the Regency-style country villa that included impressive stables built by J. S. Cartwright of Kingston in 1842.

> Mademoiselle from Armentières, parley vous,
> She hadn't been kissed for forty years, parley vous.
> The Prince of Wales was put in jail
> For riding a horse without a tail,
> Inky pinky parley vous.

The Prince of Wales, later Edward VIII, who visited Canada for the first time in 1919, is the subject of this version of "Mademoiselle from Armentières," a popular World War I song written by Gitz Rice, a native of New Glasgow, N.S. Kids in England were reciting it while jumping in 1959.

> The Temperance Pledge
>
> A pledge I make, no wine to take;
> Nor brandy red, that turns the head,
> No whisky hot, that makes the sot,
> Nor fiery rum, that ruins home,
> Nor will I sin, by drinking gin;
> Hard cider too, will never do;
> No lager beer, my heart to cheer;
> Nor sparkling ale, my face to pale.
> To quench my thirst I'll always bring,
> Cold water from the well or spring;
> So here I pledge perpetual hate,
> To all that can intoxicate.

Throughout the years innumerable Canadians have "taken the pledge," although not all teetotallers are familiar with the rhymed version of "the Pledge," as published by A. W. Chase in *Dr. Chase's Recipes* (1868).

> My father and mother were Irish,
> My father and mother were Irish,
> My father and mother were Irish,
> And I was Irish too.
>
> We kept the pig in the parlour,
> We kept the pig in the parlour,
> We kept the pig in the parlour,
> And it was Irish too.

This little song was sung in Ontario in the 1880s. It was said to be a favourite among the Irish settlers in the rural areas.

> Saturday night is my delight,
> And so is Sunday morning,
> But Sunday noon comes far too soon,
> And so does Monday morning.

That verse comes from the same area as the previous one, southern Ontario, and was recalled by Gladys M. Suggitt in *Roses and Thorns: A Goodly Heritage, The Early Days of Baddow and Area* (1972).

> Godiva was a lady who to Coventry did ride,
> To show all the villagers her fine and lily-white hide.
> The most observant man of all, an engineer of course,
> Was the only one who noticed that Godiva rode a horse.

Old engineering song, School of Practical Science, Faculty of Applied Science and Engineering, University of Toronto. The song, which is still sung, dates from the turn of the century.

> Away with tunics, cocked hats, swords
> In proof of stern endeavour
> We'll wear (where Adam wore the fig)
> The Maple Leaf for Ever.

This verse amused the Ottawa mandarins during the late 1950s, when it was decided that External Affairs officers would have to decline all foreign honours. Authorship has been attributed to the British high commissioner of the day and to a member of his staff who had a sharp tongue — and pen.

> Lives of farmers all remind us
> We must work at every chance
> And departing leave behind us
> Extra patches on our pants.

Doggerel "quoted in a budget speech of long ago," according to the poet and lawyer F. R. Scott who is vague about its provenance.

> Let's have a cheer for the academics,
> The martyrs of our generation,
> Their present youthfulness they sacrifice
> To study past degenerations!

Doggerel current in Ontario in 1975.

> There was a young woman
> Who lived in a shoe,
> She hadn't any children —
> She knew what to do.

Modern variation to the nursery rhyme about the "old woman . . . who had so many children / She didn't know what to do."

> Four and twenty Yankees, feeling very dry,
> Went across the border to get a drink of Rye.
> When the Rye was opened, the Yanks began to sing,
> "God bless America, but God save the King!"

When the Duke of Windsor (as the Prince of Wales) toured Canada in 1919, he heard this drinking song in a Canadian border town (which remains unidentified). His father, King George V, took great delight in this verse, which is to be sung to the tune of the nursery rhyme "Four and Twenty Blackbirds."

> Sing a song of sixpence,
>   A bottle full of rye,
> Four and twenty ounces
>   For a month's supply.
> When the war is over,
>   We'll all begin to sing,
> "Now we've finished Hitler,
>   Where's Mackenzie King!"

New words to the old nursery rhyme, sung at the Air Force Base, Glace Bay, N.S., 1940-45.

> He met his wife at a travel bureau,
>   And they began to court.
> She was looking for a vacation
>   And he was the last resort.
> When we come to make up the pages,
>   Sometimes the copy won't fit;
> Then we have to resort to a filler:
>   This week — THIS IS IT!

A "filler" from an Ontario weekly, 1940s.

Children's Rhymes

> Eskimo, Eskimo, Eskimo pie,
> Turn around and touch the sky.
>
> *
>
> Two little cars, two little kisses;
> Two weeks later, Mister and Missus.
>
> *
>
> Alouette-a, smoke a cigarett-a,
> Chew tobacco, spit it on the floor.
> In comes Nancy, spank her little bumbo.
> Ouch! Ouch! Ouch! Don't you do it any more.
>
> *

Christopher Columbus sailed the sea,
Huckleberry treasures all for me,
And the waves went higher, higher, higher.

*

Chungi, mungi
Chucka chicka chungi,
Alligator ungi, ohhhh!

*

Tattle tale, ginger ale,
Stick your head in a garbage pail.

Six skipping rhymes, counting-out rhymes, taunts and teases of Ontario children during the 1960s, collected by Edith Fowke in *Sally Go Round the Sun* (1969).

The twenty-fourth of May
Is the Queen's birthday;
If you don't give us a holiday,
We'll all run away.

This traditional verse has been popular since the first Empire Day in 1899. It first appeared in Sara Jeannette Duncan's novel *The Imperialist* (1904).

One, two, three, alora,
Four, five, six, alora,
Seven, eight, nine, alora,
Ten, A-Lora Secord!

Here is a ball-bouncing rhyme, current in Toronto in 1959, that recalls the heroic trek of Laura Secord during the War of 1812.

In summertime the sun shines bright
And this is not a trick —
You cannot tell the day from night.
'Cause you're in Inuvik.

This verse was composed by a pupil attending Sir Alexander Mackenzie School, Inuvik, N.W.T., 1960s.

Ghosts and Goblins,
Witches, Fairies;
Never mind it
If they're hairy.

Jump-rope rhyme of a seven-year-old girl in a North York, Ont., school, 1975.

Double-Dactyls

Higgledy-piggledy,
Hudson's Bay Company,
Maker of blanketing,
Seller of booze,

Keeps you warm outside and
Dipsomaniacally
Warms you internally
Too, if you choose.

Flibberty-gibberty,
Marshall McLunacy's
Gutenberg Galaxy
Darkens the night,

Burying messages
Under the media,
Abecedarian's
Source of delight!

Two double-dactyls (that incredibly difficult light-verse form) published in a *Maclean's* contest in July 1967. (The first is by Graeme Bacque of Toronto, the second by E. F. Miller of Vancouver.)

Bridal Gowns

Married in white, you have chosen aright;
Married in gray, you will go far away;
Married in black, you will wish yourself back;
Married in red, you will wish yourself dead;
Married in green, ashamed to be seen;
Married in blue, he will always be true;
Married in pearl, you will live in a whirl;
Married in yellow, ashamed of your fellow;
Married in brown, you will live out of town;
Married in pink, your heart will sink.

*

Wedding Day

Monday's for health;
Tuesday's for wealth;
Wednesday's the best day of all;
Thursday's for losses;
Friday's for crosses;
Saturday's no day at all.

Two wedding rhymes common in Ontario at the turn of the century.

Sneezes

Sneeze on Monday, sneeze for news;
Sneeze on Tuesday, sneeze for shoes;
Sneeze on Wednesday, sneeze for a letter;
Sneeze on Thursday, for something better;
Sneeze on Friday, sneeze for sorrow;
Sneeze on Saturday, see your love tomorrow;
Sneeze on Sunday, your safety seek,
Or Satan will have you the rest of the week.

Rhyme common in Simcoe, Ont., at the turn of the century.

The Lumberman's Alphabet

A is for Axes which all of you know,
And B is for Boys that can use them also;
C is for Chopping we do first begin,
And D is for Danger we oft-times are in.

E is for Echo that makes the woods ring,
And F is for Foreman, the boss of our gang;
G is for Grindstone we grind our axe on,
And H is for Handle so smoothily worn.

I is for Iron that marks all our pine,
And J is for Jolly boys always on time;
K is for Keen edge on our axes we keep,
And L is for Lice that keep us from sleep.

M is for Moss to chink up our camps,
And N is for Needle to mend our old pants;
O is for Owls that hoot all the night,
And P for the Pines we fall in daylight.

Q is for Quarrelling we do not allow,
And R for the Rivers our logs they do plough;
S is for Sleighs so stout and so strong;
And T is for Teams to haul them along.

U is for Use we put our teams to,
And V is for Valleys we run our roads through;
W is for Woods we leave in the spring,
So now you have heard all I have to sing.

So merry, so merry, so merry are we,
No mortal on earth is as happy as we,
Hiderry, hoderry, hiderry down,
Give the shanty boys whiskey and nothing goes wrong.

This shanty song is to be sung "with a good swing," explain Edith Fowke and Alan Mills in *Canada's Story in Song* (1965). It was patterned after an earlier "Sailor's Alphabet" and sung in Quebec and Ontario lumber camps before the turn of the century.

Tobacco

Tobacco is an Indian weed.
It from the Devil doth proceed.
It burns your pockets, scents your clothes,
And makes a chimney of your nose.

Old Dan Tucker

Old Dan Tucker was a fine old man,
Washed his face in the frying-pan,
Combed his hair with a wagon-wheel,
And died with a toothache in his heel.

Two rhymes common in Ontario at the turn of the century.

Ask why the eagle soars in air
Or builds so high his craggy nest,
Ask why the fishes love the sea —
Then ask me why I love the West.

Verse quoted by John D. Higinbotham in *When the West Was Young* (1933).

Blood on the Saddle

There was blood on the saddle
    And blood all around,
And a great big puddle
    Of blood on the ground.

The cowboy lay in it
    All covered with gore,
And he won't go riding
    No broncos no more.

Oh, pity the cowboy
    All bloody and red,
For his bronco fell on him
    And mashed in his head.

> There was blood on the saddle
>   And blood all around,
> And a great big puddle
>   Of blood on the ground.

Dr. E. A. Corbett recalls hearing a cowboy named Oklahoma Pete sing "Blood on the Saddle" on the Cochrane Ranch west of Calgary in 1905. It was later popularized by Tex Ritter.

When the Ice Worm Nests Again

There's a dusky husky maiden in the Arctic,
And she waits for me but it is not in vain,
For some day I'll put my mukluks on and ask her
If she'll wed me when the ice worms nest again.

In the land of the pale blue snow where it's ninety-nine below,
And the polar bears are roaming o'er the plain,
In the shadow of the Pole I will clasp her to my soul;
We'll be married when the ice worms nest again.

For our wedding feast we'll have seal oil and blubber;
In our kayaks we will roam the bounding main;
All the walruses will look at us and rubber;
We'll be married when the ice worms nest again.

When some night at half-past two I return to my igloo,
After sitting with a friend who was in pain,
She'll be waiting for me there with the hambone of a bear,
And she'll beat me till the ice worms nest again.

No one remembers who wrote or first sang "When the Ice Worms Nest Again," but it first appeared in print in 1939 and may be a popular version of a verse written by Robert W. Service, "the Bard of the Yukon." An ice worm is "a stick of stained spaghetti with two red ink spots for eyes" used to scare newcomers to the Yukon. The above version of the lyrics comes from *Canada's Story in Song* (1965), by Edith Fowke and Alan Mills.

I Never Shall Forget the Day
Columbus Landed Here

I never shall forget the day
 Columbus landed here.
Myself and forty Indians
 Were there right on the pier.
He asked me why the Indians
 Wore feathers on their head.
"Oh! that's to keep their trousers up!"
 And this is what I said:

'Twas I who built the Rockies up
 And placed them where they are,
Sold whiskey to the Indians,
 Behind my little bar,
'Twas I that made Niagara Falls,
 And first discovered beer.
Oh! that was long before Columbus
 Landed over here.

Columbus asked me where to go
 To catch the China train,
I saw the poor boy had got
 The itching foot again.
Says I, "Too bad! There is no train
 That leaves for there today.
You'll find a Chinese laundryman
 Not half a block away."

'Twas I who built the Rockies up
 And placed them where they are,
Sold whiskey to the Indians,
 Behind my little bar,
'Twas I that made Niagara Falls,
 And first discovered beer.
Oh! that was long before Columbus
 Landed over here.

He saw that some of my Red Men
 Had skins that were quite fair,

And thought some other white man must
   Have wandered over there.
Says I, "You have to bear in mind
   That I've been here some time.
They certainly can not be yours,
   But they, no doubt, are mine!"

The great collector of folksongs, Marius Barbeau, identifies "I Never Shall Forget the Day" as being "partly traditional in southern British Columbia," 1908. He gave credit to Douglas Leechman for preserving the silly song.

Mad Ads

"What is the difference between unethical and ethical advertising?" asked the Arctic explorer Vilhjalmur Stefansson. "Unethical advertising uses falsehoods to deceive the public; ethical advertising uses truth to deceive the public." The following items which appeared in the personal or classified columns of Canadian daily newspapers were meant to deceive no one.

> For sale — one home-made coffin. Never been used. Fit 6'2". Reason for selling: Improved health. Phone 97937. Bill Kinnear.

The Saskatoon Star-Phoenix, June 30, 1945.

Lady who likes to talk, drink reasonably, have a pleasant time, wishes to meet a gentleman who likes to talk, drink reasonably, have a pleasant time. Purpose: talk, drink reasonably and have a pleasant time. Box 153.

The Ottawa Citizen, November 1962.

Lady seeks intelligent male companion around 45. No civil servants.

The Ottawa Citizen, June 1965.

Hunting cabins. Hemmingford area. No licence required shoot farm children, farm animals. Box M3130.

The Montreal Star, November 8, 1969.

Beautiful wedding gown, size 14. Never worn. Half price.

The Kitchener-Waterloo Record, spring,1973.

The following classified ad appeared, without telephone number or box number, in *The Canadian Forum*, November-December 1974.

> Actor must get revenge. Don't call him, he'll call you.

Revenge was not the motive behind the following advertisement that appeared complete with misprint:

PRINTING HOUSE

> The undersigned have recently been enabled to make great additions to their printing machinery and stock of tpye.

The advertisement was signed M. Longmoore & Co., Printing House, 67 Great St. James St., Montreal, and was dated 1867. The firm is no longer in business.

> Young man, driving a blue Pinto, looking for an attractive girl with black hair that I have seen driving a small greenish Japanese car at the stoplight at Bayview & Steeles, please contact me at Box 1483.

The Globe and Mail, April 30, 1973.

> Funeral director wanted, in growing city one hour from Toronto. Fifty calls a year (can be tripled).

The Toronto Star, January 29, 1975.

FOR SALE
Twin Beds — One Hardly Used

Advertisement reportedly seen in a prairie newspaper, 1930s.

OIL CLOTHS

> If King Edward and Queen Alexandra were living in Canada they would not hesitate to recommend your buying Oil Cloths made by The Dominion Oil Cloth Co., Limited.

Patriotism and profit were served by this full-page ad in *Dry Goods Review,* June 1902, a Toronto trade magazine.

THE RIOT ACT
IS NEVER
READ IN VICTORIA
Households where ladies use White Swan Cleanser.
Everything is Clean, Neat and Orderly.

This advertisement was published in *The Victoria Colonist* in May of 1915.

PART-TIME WOMEN
WANTED FOR CASHIERS

Sign in a Loblaw's store in Toronto, 1960s.

OUR WORMS TRY HARDER

Sign at a bait outlet in the Okanagan region of British Columbia, 1970s.

FOR SALE

800 acres highly improved stock farm, located on Pelletier Creek. Would sell on cash instalment basis. If interested write Fred Hearsey, Duncairn, Sask. N.B. I might be tempted to trade this farm for something really useful, say some white mice or goldfish, or even a playful little monkey. F.H.

Classified advertisement placed by Fred Hearsey, a hard-pressed but witty farmer, in a Saskatchewan newspaper during the 1930s, according to James H. Gray in *The Winter Years* (1966).

N.B.

To be let, or to be sold, for the term of her life,
Elizabeth Hall — by the way of a wife;
She's old and she's ugly, ill-natured and thin.
For further particulars enquire within.

Notice (said to be humorous) in *The Upper Canada Almanack for the Year 1837*.

BLURB FOR A BOOK THAT BARES ALL

A bizarre world in which intercourse precedes introduction . . . pleasure follows perversion . . . beating is followed by bestiality! Read for yourself the whole story of "O"!

Ultra-dramatic blurb to promote a book, concocted by S. J. Potts of Port Arthur, Ont. Mr. Potts won the top prize of $25 for submitting this to a *Maclean's* contest in 1968. (The book the blurb describes? *The Concise Oxford English Dictionary*!)

What is Dress?

What is Dress, let me ask? for I cannot suppose,
    When I hear the word Dress, that it merely means clothes;
No; style, make and quality have much to do
    With the meaning of Dress, and I'll prove it is true;
If a garment surprisingly good you behold,
    And where was it bought, at SMART's you'll be told —
If a garment you see in which style is displayed,
    On enquiring you'll find at SMART's 'twas made;
Or if in a garment you happen to see
    Superior workmanship, SMART's it will be.
In price, too, you'll find that of him you can buy
    The cheapest of clothes, which the trade can supply,
Now, there are some thousands who make and sell clothes.
    Yet we never even hear a whisper of those,
For go where you will, or whoever you see,
    If a name you hear mentioned, SMART's it will be,
Do you ask why it is, it is easy to guess,
    'Tis because SMART surpasses all others in dress;
'Tis because he's determined his clothes shall possess
    Those first-rate essentials which constitute dress.

This advertisement for T. Smart, Tailor and Clothier, Brockville, Ont., appeared in *Brockville Almanac for the Year of Our Lord 1868; Being Leap Year*. He was a sharp fellow with a rhyme.

I, Joseph Sobotka, declare that I never said that Frank Hermonskay poisoned his wife's mother, and that if ever I did say anything that might be construed in such a way I am sorry for it. I further say that I had no evidence that such was the case and express my regret for any trouble Mr. or Mrs. Hermonskay have had and I withdraw any unkind words I ever used and hope Mr. Hermonskay will accept this apology and trust we shall hereafter be good friends and I will pay all costs Mr. Hermonskay has been put to in this case. (Signed) Joe Sobotka.

Classified advertisement in *Esterhazy Observer and Pheasant Hills Advertiser*, Esterhazy, Sask., March 21, 1907. (This ad was spotted by Don Willmott and is a "Metro Morning" prize-winner.)

Subscribe, Don't Borrow

Once upon a time a nickle-nurser sent his kid to borrow the neighbour's paper, and the kid upset a hive of bees, and was soon covered with bumps.

His father ran to help him and caught his chin on a clothesline and sprained his back and fell and broke an $85 watch. The clothes pole fell over the car and smashed the windshield, and mother, rushing out to see what occasioned all the excitement, upset a gallon churn of cream into a basket of kittens, drowning them all.

The electric iron burned through the ironing board whilst she was out of the kitchen, setting fire to the house, and the firemen broke all the windows and chopped a hole in the roof. The baby ate a jar of pickles and got cholera mortus and the doctor's bill was $15.

The daughter ran away with the hired man during the excitement, the dog bit the neighbour's kid and the calves ate the tail off four nightshirts on the clothesline.

Moral — Subscribe to your hometown paper. Don't borrow it!!!

This homily from *The Grenfell Sun* dates from 1926 and is reproduced by J. George Johnston in *The Weeklies: Biggest Circulation in Town* (1972).

The World of Business

"We are not manufacturers merely of articles of wood and stone, and iron and cotton and wool, and so on; we manufacture enthusiasms; we manufacture Canadian sentiment; we manufacture a feeling of pride in our country, and we manufacture a spirit of independence, a spirit of national pride." So wrote Cirus A. Birge, president of the Canadian Manufacturer's Association. When he made those observations in 1903, Birge did not have in mind the following "enthusiasms."

FEATHER YOUR NEST WITH A LITTLE DOWN

Furniture store, Barrie, Ont., 1949.

IF YOUR CLOTHES ARE NOT BECOMING TO YOU,
YOU SHOULD BE COMING TO US

Tailor shop, Montreal, 1950.

MR. ALEX WILL CURL UP AND DYE FOR YOU

Mr. Alex Hair Design Salon, Kingston, Ont., 1972.

DRIVE CAREFULLY — BLOOD'S HARD TO REMOVE

Drycleaning establishment, Kitchener, Ont., 1972.

DROP YOUR PANTS HERE . . .
YOU WILL RECEIVE IMMEDIATE ATTENTION

Drycleaning establishment, Waterloo, Ont., 1973.

CLOSED FOR THE SEASON
REASON?   FREEZIN'!

Drive-in theatre, New Glasgow, N.S., October 1972.

NO WASHEE —
NO PARKEE

Limited-space parking lot, King Koin launderette, Ottawa, 1970.

SPECIAL
1972 MODEL AS NEW, OWNED AND USED
BY DOCTOR TO MAKE HOUSE CALLS

Sign on late-model car on a used-car lot, Hamilton, Ont., 1972.

OUR BUSINESS IS GOING DOWNHILL

Ski-supply store, Kingston, Ont., 1972.

GO AHEAD AND LOSE YOUR COOL!

Motto of Smith-Webasto Heating Systems, Toronto, 1973.

PART-TIME BOY WANTED FOR EXPANDING BUSINESS.
EXPERIENCE ABSOLUTELY NECESSARY,
BUT NOT ESSENTIAL.

Sign in a shoe repair shop, in an ethnic area of Montreal, 1940s; Mordecai Richler regards this as his favourite sign.

OPEN DAY AND NIGHT
We Never Clothe

Sign allegedly posted at the entrance to a nudist camp near Barrie, Ont., 1960s.

Available
EXTRA LARGE BACHELORS

Sign outside a new apartment building, Mississauga, Ont., 1970.

EDIFICE WRECKS

Sign (in Old English script) on a junkyard near Picton, Ont., 1974.

Don't run into debt —
Buy a car and ride into it!

Sign observed in a used-car lot, Edmonton, Alta., 1974.

LORNE'S
SECOND HAND
ANTIQUES

Sign above a store on Highway 35 between Norland and Coboconk, Ont., 1975.

EYES EXAMINED
CLOSED

Optician's window, after hours, Calgary, 1950s.

SALVATION NAVY

Name of an antique store, Toronto, 1965.

JACK HIMSELF
From Soup to Nuts

Name and motto of the proprietor of a junk shop in Toronto, 1965.

ANTIQUES & JUNQUE

Antique shop, Peterborough, Ont., 1968.

HELP BEAUTIFY JUNKYARDS
Throw Something Lovely Away To-Day!
Help Satisfy Our Scrap-e-tiet

Sign outside a Toronto junk yard, observed by Marshall McLuhan, 1968.

EAT HERE OR WE ALL STARVE

Sign in the window of a greasy spoon on Highway 2 near Hamilton, mid-1930s.

A classic piece of Canadiana is "The Rules and Regulations of the Fort Macleod Hotel." The proprietor of the Alberta hotel, Henry "Kamoose" Taylor, was a former whisky-trader whose Indian nickname is said to mean "wife-stealer." Taylor's rules were posted in the lobby of his hotel and recalled half a century later by John D. Higinbotham.

MACLEOD HOTEL RULES AND REGULATIONS
(Adopted unanimously by the Proprietor, September 1, 1882 A.D.)

Guests will be provided with breakfast and dinner, but must rustle their own lunch.

Spiked boots and spurs must be removed at night before retiring.

Dogs are not allowed in the Bunks, but may sleep underneath.

Candles, hot water and other luxuries charged extra, also towels and soap.

Towels changed weekly. Insect Powder for sale at the bar.

Crap, Chuck Luck, Stud Horse Poker and Black Jack games are run by the management. Indians and niggers charged double rates.

Special Rates to "Gospel Grinders" and the "Gambling Perfesh."

Every known fluid (water excepted) for sale at the bar.

A deposit must be made before towels, soap or candles can be carried to rooms. When boarders are leaving, a rebate will be made on all candles or parts of candles not burned or eaten.

Two or more persons must sleep in one bed when so requested by the proprietor.

Not more than one dog allowed to be kept in each single room.

Baths furnished free down at the river, but bathers must furnish their own soap and towels.

No kicking regarding the quality or quantity of meals will be allowed; those who do not like the provender will get out, or be put out.

Assaults on the cook are strictly prohibited.

Quarrelsome or boisterous persons, also those who shoot off without provocation guns or other explosive weapons on the premises, and all boarders who get killed, will not be allowed to remain in the House.

When guests find themselves or their baggage thrown

over the fence, they may consider that they have received notice to quit.

Jewelry and other valuables will not be locked in the safe. This hotel has no such ornament as a safe.

The proprietor will not be accountable for anything.

In case of FIRE the guests are requested to escape without unnecessary delay.

The BAR in the Annex will be open day and night. All Day drinks, 50 cents each; Night drinks, $1.00 each. No Mixed Drinks will be served except in case of death in the family.

Only regularly registered guests will be allowed the special privilege of sleeping on the Bar Room floor.

Guests without baggage must sleep in the vacant lot, and board elsewhere until their baggage arrives.

Guests are forbidden to strike matches or spit on the ceiling, or to sleep in bed with their boots on.

No cheques cashed for anybody. Payment must be made in Cash, Gold Dust, or Blue Chips.

Saddle horses can be hired at any hour of the Day or Night, or the next day or night if necessary.

Meals served in own rooms will not be guaranteed in any way. Our waiters are hungry and not above temptation.

To attract attention of waiters or bell boys, shoot a hole through the door panel. Two shots for ice water, three for a deck of cards, and so on.

All guests are requested to rise at 6 A.M. This is imperative as the sheets are needed for tablecloths.

No tips must be given to any waiters or servants. Leave them all with the proprietor, and he will distribute them if it is considered necessary.

Everything Cash in Advance. Following Tariff subject to change:

Board — $25.00 per month.

Board and Lodging — $50.00 per month, with wooden bench to sleep on.

Board and Lodging — $60.00 per month, with bed to sleep on.

Our Graffiti

There is a reference in the Old Testament to "the handwriting on the wall." Canadian graffiti has little to do with Biblical prophecy, as these specimens prove.

BEHOLD THE POPE OF CANADA AND THE ENGLISH SOT!

This early specimen of graffiti was found painted across the statue of King George III, in Place d'Armes, Montreal, May 1, 1755. This was to protest the passage of the Quebec Act, and the culprit was said to be Thomas Walker, a pro-American merchant living in Montreal who shortly thereafter left Quebec for the American colonies under the cover of night.

NO ALIENS!

This succinct message was written on fences in chalk and white paint in York (now Toronto), 1827-28. It is a nineteenth-century version of "Yankee Go Home."

NO ORIENTALS NEED APPLY

Common in British Columbia before the turn of the century.

NO ENGLISHMEN NEED APPLY

Common in eastern Canada and the prairies in the first decade of this century.

BLEED
YOUR KING AND COUNTRY ~~NEED~~ YOU

Defaced war poster, Saint John, N.B., during the First World War.

UP THE POPE!

Anti-papist message observed on a wall in Quebec City, 1964.

UP THE QUEEN. NO POPE HERE.

Added to the above anti-papist message, Quebec City, 1964.

VIVE ELISABETH . . . TAYLOR!

Signs displayed during the royal visit of Queen Elizabeth, Quebec City, fall, 1964.

VISIT/EZ EXPO?
VISIT/EZ LES SLUMS!

Bilingual admonition, painted on Montreal walls during the Centennial year when Expo 67 was in full swing.

CENT ANS D'INJUSTICE

Separatist slogan, "One hundred years of injustice," painted on walls, Quebec City, 1967.

> To do is to be — Jean-Paul Sartre
> To be is to do — Bertrand Russell
> Do be do be do — Frank Sinatra

Scribbled on a latrine wall, York University, Toronto, 1969.

McLUHAN READS BOOKS

Elaborately lettered in Old English script on the wall of the Centre for Culture and Technology, University of Toronto, spring, 1969. The Centre is directed by media apologist, Marshall McLuhan.

WHAT CANADA NEEDS NOW
IS A NORTHROP FRYE COLOURING BOOK

Graffiti referring to the distinguished literary critic, washroom wall, University College, University of Toronto, 1973.

LAKE ERIE DIED FOR YOUR SINS

Printed on a wall at the University of Michigan, Ann Arbor, Michigan, 1970.

KEEP YOUR CITY CLEAN — EAT A PIGEON

Added to the wall of the Sun Life Building, Montreal, 1972.

CANADA IS TOO RICH TO BE POOR

Graffiti on a wall during a Canada Day celebration, Port Colborne, Ont., 1972.

THIS CHEWING GUM TASTES LIKE RUBBER

Message scratched on the side of a prophylactic-dispensing machine in the men's room of a gas station in Hope, B.C., 1971.

PREVENT LOCKJAW — OPEN YOUR MOUTH

Written on a blackboard (by an exasperated professor, no doubt), Simon Fraser University, Burnaby, B.C., 1965.

STALIN'S GRAVE IS A COMMUNIST PLOT

Observed on a washroom wall in a Winnipeg meeting hall, 1972.

AN APPLE A DAY KEEPS THE DOCTOR AWAY —
BUT BABIES ARE THE RESULT OF GREEN PAIRS

Graffiti on the wall of the Pauline Johnson Collegiate, Brantford, Ont., 1973.

58% OF ALL DEATHS ARE FATAL

Another specimen of graffiti from the students of Pauline Johnson Collegiate, Brantford, Ont., 1973.

PUBLISH OR PRAIRIES!

Found printed on a blackboard in a classroom at York University, Toronto, 1973.

> IMMANUEL KANT
> but
> KUBLA KHAN
> if
> SHAKESPEARE WILL
> should
> WILLIAM TELL?

From a washroom wall, North York Public Library, Toronto, 1975.

> NECROPHILIA MEANS NEVER HAVING TO SAY YOU'RE SORRY

Graffiti, wall of men's washroom, Grossman's Tavern, Toronto, 1974.

> RENE LEVESQUE BUYS CANADA SAVINGS BONDS

Wall writing from Carleton University, Ottawa, 1974.

> JESUS SAVES,
> KEON GETS THE REBOUND
> HE SHOOTS! HE SCORES!

Inscribed on a washroom wall, Toronto, 1973.

> THE MOVING HAND . . . MISSPELLS

*

> SUZANNE RUSSELL WAS HERE AND GOT SMART AND LEFT

*

> NIXON HAS V.D. (THAT'S BULLSHIT ABOUT THE BLOODCLOTS)

Student's Administrative Council, University of Toronto, 1975.

> TERRY HOROLUK IS INSECURE

Graffiti, Winnipeg Art School wall, 1965.

> FIGHT LIKE HELL FOR PACIFISM!

Graffiti, washroom, Vancouver bar, 1966.

> WHATEVER HAPPENED TO . . . NOSTALGIA?

Written on the wall of the women's washroom in the Embassy Tavern, Toronto, 1975.

> YOU'D THINK, TO READ ALL THIS WIT,
> OLD BILL HIMSELF CAME HERE TO SHIT!

Scribbled beneath some unpublishable graffiti on a W.C. wall, Festival Theatre, Stratford, Ont., late 1960s.

> TIME IS NATURE'S WAY OF KEEPING EVERYTHING
> FROM HAPPENING AT ONCE

Wall wisdom from a Toronto lavatory, 1975.

> CROMBIE IS A MENTAL MIDGET

Graffiti alluding to the height of Toronto's "tiny perfect mayor," David Crombie, fall, 1974.

> JESUS SAVES
> BUT MOSES INVESTS

Written on a garage door, Inuvik, N.W.T., 1974.

> EXEGESIS SAVES

From a Toronto lavatory wall, 1975.

> FIGHTING FOR PEACE IS LIKE FUCKING FOR VIRGINITY

Women's washroom, York University, Toronto, 1974.

> SISYPHUS IS A PUSHER

Men's washroom, York University, Toronto, 1974.

Readers of *Maclean's* were asked to copy down and send to the magazine their favourite graffiti. These were published in the issue of December 3, 1966. Here are some of the best.

> CHICKEN LITTLE WAS RIGHT.

MILTON CAN'T RELATE TO HIS ENVIRONMENT.

*

GIVE YOUR CHILDREN SOME MENTAL BLOCKS FOR CHRISTMAS.

*

OUR GOD IS ALIVE; SORRY TO HEAR ABOUT YOURS.

*

ZEUS SAVES.

*

DANIEL JOHNSON EATS ENGLISH MUFFINS.

*

FREE TIM BUCK.

*

HETEROSEXUALITY IS COMING BACK [Added: WHAT'S THAT?]

*

PABLUM: BREAKFAST OF HAS-BEENS.

*

HELP STAMP OUT VOLKSWAGENS — USE RAID.

*

HELP PREVENT EARTHQUAKES.

*

REPEAL THE LAW OF GRAVITY.

*

HELP A NUN KICK HER HABIT!

*

I'VE GOT LEPROSY — WHAT'S EATING YOU?

*

THE PUBLIC BE JAMMED. [Fingerpainted in dirt on the side of a Vancouver bus]

*

KEEP B.C. GREEN. PLANT MARIJUANA. [Scrawled on a fire-warning sign in a B.C. forest]

*

HELP! I'M BEING HELD PRISONER IN THIS ROCK. [Scribbled on a boulder in northern Ontario]

ANYONE CAUGHT WRITING ON THIS WALL
WILL BE SENT TO MACLEAN'S

Graffiti from the washroom wall of the editorial offices of *Saturday Night* magazine, reported in 1966 by Claude X. Labrecque.

Bumpers & Buttons

No book of contemporary humour would be complete without a section devoted to those two contemporary forms of self-expression, bumper-stickers and lapel buttons.

The ubiquitous bumper-sticker has been called a "mobile billboard." The most common ones testify that the owner of the automobile whose bumper they brighten has been fortunate enough to behold NIAGARA FALLS, or wealthy enough to visit DISNEYLAND. Less common are the zany and witty (and sometimes manic) ones reproduced here.

The lapel button, like the bumper-sticker, is manufactured rather than handmade, and its message is standardized and sometimes of a quasi-official nature. Surprisingly popular during 1975 has been the WHY NOT? button, this country's contribution to International Women's Year. (Credit for the cryptic slogan has been claimed by a male — Dalton Camp.) The wearer of a lapel button has the choice of the message he wishes to buy and flash to the world. Lapel buttons and bumper-stickers have been called "specimens of urban folklore." They are kind of silly, but fun.

Bumper-stickers

HONK YOUR HORN IF YOU LOVE JESUS
Evangelical bumper-sticker, common in Ontario, 1968.

UNEMPLOYMENT ISN'T WORKING
Labour bumper-sticker promoted by the United Auto Workers, Toronto, 1974.

MILK DRINKERS ARE GOOD LOVERS
Observed in Peterborough, Ont., March 1974.

IF YOU CAN READ THIS, YOU'RE TOO DAMN CLOSE!
The perennial bumper-sticker, common across Canada throughout the 1960s.

LET THOSE EASTERN BASTARDS FREEZE IN THE DARK
Bumper-sticker observed in Calgary during the oil crisis of 1973.

THAT EASTERN BASTARD IS MY BROTHER
Bumper-sticker issued by the mayor of Calgary to protest the previous one, October 1973.

SUPPORT POLLUTION: VOTE SOCIAL CREDIT
Bumper-sticker seen in Edmonton, Alta., during the provincial election, 1971.

MAFIA STAFF CAR
Keep Offa the Handsa
Bumper-sticker noted in Toronto in 1975.

READ BOOKS NOT BUMPER STICKERS
Bumper-sticker publicizing Edmonton Book Week, November 1974.

CANADA IS ALIVE AND REAL
Bumper-sticker, Toronto, May 1975.

I CAN'T BARRETT
Bumper-sticker critical of B.C. Premier Dave Barrett, observed in Kamloops, spring, 1974.

REPEAL BANANAS
Bumper-sticker observed in Toronto, January 1974. Apparently a protest against protests!

NIRVANA IS NEEDED.

*

LOVE IS A MANY GENDERED THING.

*

SUPPORT YOUR LOCAL POET.

*

TAKE LSD AND SEE.

*

WHERE IS LEE HARVEY OSWALD NOW THAT WE REALLY NEED HIM?

*

RELEASE OSCAR WILDE.

*

WILLIAM DAVIS FOR EX-PREMIER.

*

STOP OXFAM AND FEED TWIGGY.

*

I AM A HUMAN BEING; DO NOT FOLD, SPINDLE OR MUTILATE.

*

UNBUTTON.

Messages on buttons observed across Canada during the late sixties and early seventies.

OTTO LANG IS TWO FOUR-LETTER WORDS.

Message on a button worn by a women's libber who did not care for the anti-abortion stand of the federal minister of Justice, January 1975.

From See to Saw

"From See to Saw" may not be the motto of Canada (that distinction belongs to "From Sea to Sea") but it does describe the contents of this section. Here is literary and sub-literary material from across Canada, from the past and present. Most of it is inadvertently amusing.

> TO RESTORE FROM STROKE OF LIGHTNING. — Shower with cold water for two hours; if the patient does not show signs of life, put salt in the water, and continue to shower an hour longer.

This piece of medical advice comes from the good ladies of "Toronto and Chief Cities and Towns of Canada" who compiled *The Canadian Home Cook Book* (1877).

> MOTOR VEHICLE LAWS
>
> Every motor vehicle shall be equipped with an alarm bell, gong or horn, and the same shall be sounded whenever it shall be reasonably necessary to notify pedestrians or others of its approach.

This law was on the Ontario statute books in 1920, according to R.F.C.C. Barfett in *Highways and Byways of Ontario* (1923).

> The Emperor Napoleon III has decided to invite the Canadian Press Association to Paris. They will be entertained at dinner at St. Cloud, if they do not arrive on Wednesday, which is washing day.

News item, July 15, 1868, quoted by Governor General Jules Léger in an address at the Annual Dinner, Canadian Press, Toronto, May 1, 1974.

Clem

"There was a Canadian counterpart to Kilroy, a mythical Clem," explains Robert Reisner in his amusing study *Graffiti: Two Thousand Years of Wall Writing* (1974). "His name was inscribed in every unlikely place in the army camps. At one command post, it drove the officer in charge to a point of extreme irritation. One morning he called out every single man in the camp to assemble, averred in strong language that the inscription must cease, dismissed them, and returned to his office — to find 'Wot! No Clem?' inscribed on his desk."

TREASURY BOARD COMMANDMENTS

1. Thou shalt have no other gods before the Treasury Board.

2. Thou shalt not bow down thyself to any other board or council nor serve them; for we of the Treasury Board are a jealous god visiting the iniquities of the fathers upon the children and showing mercy to those who keep our commandments.

3. Thou shalt not take the name of the Treasury Board in vain.

4. Remember the Budget Day to keep it holy.

5. Honour thy father and thy mother, the Minister of Finance, and the president of the Treasury Board.

6. Thou shalt not kill any government department or agency.

7. Thou shalt not commit adultery with the universities.

8. Thou shalt not steal any authority or control.

9. Thou shalt not bear witness against the Department of Industry, Trade and Commerce.

10. Thou shalt not covet the prerogatives of other ministers.

This specimen of contemporary Ottawa urban-lore was reproduced (with a chuckle) by F. Ronald Hayes in *The Chaining of Prometheus: Evolution of a Power Structure for Canadian Science* (1973).

Cwick Canada Cwiz
(Questions)

1. What's the capital of Canada?
2. What's the automotive capital of Canada?
3. What has become of the Canadian protest movement?
4. How do they take the census in Canada?
5. What is a Canadian political cartoon?
6. What is a hard-hitting Canadian political cartoon?
7. Why is it better to shop in Toronto than in Saskatoon?
8. Why is Canada always pink on the map?

(Answers)

1. Mainly American.
2. Detroit.
3. He got married and settled down.
4. Take the American census and divide by ten.
5. A beaver rolling up its sleeves.
6. A beaver rolling up its sleeves and making a fist.
7. You can order direct from New York.
8. From embarrassment.

The above quiz graced the pages of *National Lampoon*, April 1973. The American humour magazine devoted an issue to this country. The editors called the issue "Canada: The Retarded Giant on Your Doorstep." One article in the issue was titled "Canada: Consider the Alternative."

Questionnaire

Is virginity obsolete?
   Not yet.
What is meant by the double standard?
   I haven't the faintest idea.
Why isn't there a pill for men?
   Yeah, why isn't there?
What gave you most of the information you presently have on the topic of sex education?
   Myself.
Is the pill difficult to obtain?
   Not difficult enough.
What is an I.U.D.?
   Interviral Urinal Devise.
How does the diaphragm, as a method of birth control, function?
   Helps push baby out.
What is the population of Port Credit?
   Increasing.
Why don't human beings produce litters?
   Because they aren't four-legged creatures.
Deformed babies should be allowed to live.
   True.

How effective is the condom?
Not so effective because it could up and leak.
Use the remaining paper to list some of the areas you feel should be discussed.
All of them.

"Questions and answers culled from a questionnaire given to a Grade XI class at the start of a unit on Birth Control and Family Planning at Humberside Collegiate Institute" in Toronto, quoted by Loren Jay Lind in *The Learning Machine: A Hard Look at Toronto Schools* (1974).

What to Teach Girls

The following rules (what to teach girls) have been compiled by an eminent woman of the present day. Teach them thoroughly, she says, the following important things, and there will be more happy women:

Teach them how to make shirts.
Teach them not to wear false hair.
Teach them not to powder and paint.
Teach them not to run up store bills.
Teach them to wash and iron clothes.
Teach them to make their own dresses.
Teach them to wear thick, warm shoes.
Teach them self-reliance and independence.
Teach them how to make bread and cook well.
Teach them that a dollar is only a hundred cents.
Teach them to darn stockings and sew on buttons.
Teach them to say no, and mean it, or yes, and stick to it.
Teach them to wear calico dresses and not feel ashamed of them.
Teach them that a good, rosy romp is worth fifty dyspeptics or consumptives.
Teach them to regard the morals and not the money of their beaux.
Teach them to keep house in good order, with everything in its place.

Teach them to have nothing to do with intemperate and dissolute young men.

Teach them that the more one lives within one's income, the more one will save.

Teach them that tight lacing ought to be prevented by law, as opium smoking is in China.

Teach them that the further one gets beyond one's income, the nearer one gets to the poor-house.

Teach them that a reliable young man with good working or business qualities is worth a hundred loafers in fine harness.

Teach them every day some item of dry, hard, practical common sense, and they will yet find time for idealism.

Teach them that any amount of tight lacing and pinching of corns cannot improve a form that the Almighty made in His own image.

Give them, if possible, a good, substantial education, and as many of the accomplishments as you can afford, but never neglect their home training.

These do's and don't's were directed at yesterday's women — the grandmothers and great-grandmothers of today's women's libbers. The passage comes from *The Pembroke Observer and Upper Ottawa Advertiser*, Friday, May 28, 1880.

This I have never seen. — I have never seen such hard times as the present in all my life. I have never seen an old maid decidedly opposed to matrimony. I have never seen a pretty girl that did not know it. I have never seen a lawyer refuse a fee on account of his client's poverty. I have never seen a woman that was tongue tied. I have never seen rich men prefer marrying poor girls. I have never seen but one lady use a bed wrench and pin to tighten her corsets. I have never seen a woman die with lock jaw.

From *The Upper Canada Almanack for the Year 1837*.

"For the Old Ladies"
Proverbs popular in Montreal (1850s)

A tea-party without a scandal is like a knife without a handle.

*

Words without deeds are like the husks without the seeds.

*

Features without grace are like a clock without a face.

*

A land without the laws is like a cat without her claws.

*

Life without cheer is like a cellar without beer.

*

A master without a cane is like a rider without a rein.

*

Marriage without means is like a horse without his beans.

*

A man without a wife is like a fork without a knife.

The following four-line verse was found on a slip of paper between the pages of *Fourth Book of Lessons, for the Use of Schools*, a primary-school reader published in Montreal in 1853:

I'm one of those girls not afraid of the men,
And would as soon be romping as spinning,
And if they do steal a kiss now and then,
I'm sure it's not very great sinning.

With Confederation in 1867 came the first readers, the so-called "Canadian Series of School Books." The following two lessons open the *First Book of Reading Lessons* (1867):

Lesson I.

is it an ox?
it is an ox.
so it is an ox.
am I on it? no.
is an ox on it? no.
is an ox in it?
an ox is in it.

Lesson II.

do we see an ass?
we do see an ass.
is it an ox?
no, it is an ass.
is he on it? he is on.
see it go!
go on, ass, do go on.
do we go to it?
no. we go by it, so.

Albertus Magnus's Egyptian Secrets
(for the Benefit of Mankind)

To Make Yourself Invisible

Pierce the right eye of a bat,
and carry it with you,
and you will be invisible.

To Compel a Dog, Horse or Other Animal to Follow You

"Caspar guide thee,
 Balthasar bind thee,
 Melchior keep thee,"
three times.
These words utter
into the right ear.

An Ambrose-Stone

Steal the eggs of a raven,
boil them hard,
lay them again into the nest
and the raven will fly across the sea
and bring a stone from abroad
and lay it over the eggs
and they will become at once soft again.

If such a stone is wrapped up
into a bay leaf
and is given to a prisoner,
that prisoner will be
liberated at once.
Whoever touches a door with such a stone,
to him that door will be opened,
and he who puts that stone into his mouth
will understand the song of every bird.

To See What Others Cannot See

Take a cat's eye,
lay it in salt water,
let it remain there for three days,
and then for six days
into the rays of the sun,
after this have it set in silver,
and hang it around your neck.

That No Person Will Deny Anything To You

Take a rooster, three years old,
throw it into a new earthen pot,
and pierce it through,
then put it into an ant's hill,
and let it remain until the ninth day thereafter,
then take it out again
and you will find in its head a white stone,
which you must carry on your person,
and then nobody will deny you anything.

To Prevent Every Person from Hitting the Target

Put a splinter of wood
which has been hit by a thunder bolt
behind the target.
No person will be able to hit such a target.

To Cause Rifles and Muskets to Miss Fire

Speak these words:
"AFA AFCA NOSTRA,"
when you are able to look
into the barrel of some person's gun
and it will fail to discharge;
but if you desire it to give fire
recall these words backward.

*To Burn a Witch so that She Receives Pock Marks
Over Her Entire Body*

Take butter from the household larder,
render it down in an iron pan until it boils,
then take ivy or wintergreen, and fry it;
take three nails of a coffin and stick them in that sauce;
carry the mass to a place where neither sun nor moon shines
    into,
and the witch will be sick for half a year.

For Freckles

When persons have freckles,
catch the dew that settles on wheat,
mix with rose-water and oil of lilies.
With this water wash the face.
It drives all the freckles away,
and adds to the beauty of the face
by improving the complexion.

For a Toothache

Take a new, but useless nail.
Pick the teeth well with it,
till they are bleeding.
Then take the nail,
and drive it into a rafter,
toward the rising sun,
where neither sun nor moon shines,
and speak, at the first stroke,
"Toothache, vanish";
  at the second stroke,

"Toothache, banish";
at the third stroke,
"Toothache, thither fly."

*A Magic for One Who Has Been Infatuated
by Illicit Love to a Female*

Such a person must put a pair of shoes on,
and walk therein until his feet perspire,
but must walk fast, so that the feet do not smell badly;
then take off the right shoe,
drink some beer or wine out of this shoe,
and he will from that moment
lose all affection for her.

To Try if a Person is Chaste

Sap of radish squeezed into the hand
will prove what you wish to know.
If they do not fumble or grabble
they are all right.

How to Cause Your Intended Wife to Love You

Take a turtle-dove tongue into your mouth,
talk to your friend agreeably,
kiss her,
and she will love you so dearly
that she cannot love another.

The preceding recipes, spells, curses, incantations and enchantments come from a curious book that, while not Canadian in origin, has been widely read — and used — in parts of Canada. The book is *Albertus Magnus: Being the Approved, Verified, Sympathetic and Natural Egyptian Secrets — or — White and Black Art for Man and Beast, Revealing the Forbidden Knowledge of Ancient Philosophers.* This all-but-forgotten tome is employed in German parts of the country, especially in Waterloo County, the Mennonite district of Ontario, and is rumoured to be consulted from time to time, as required, by farmers and elders of the community. The spells have been reproduced as they appear in *Albertus Magnus*, but the lines of prose have not been permitted to run to the edges of the pages — just in case!

Excerpts from
"Humberside Waiting Room"
* Joke Book *
Toronto Junction, 1900
Price 1¢.

Man's inhumanity to man makes countless lawyers happy.

*

Johnny: Pa! Are Kings and Queens always good?
Pa: Not always, my boy; not when there are aces out against them.

*

[To the School Maids of Toronto Junction]
May they add virtue to beauty; subtract envy from friendship; multiply amiable accomplishments by sweetness of temper; divide time by sociability and economy, and reduce scandal to its lowest denomination.

Metric Maxims
(with apologies to the Metric Commission)

A milligram of prevention is worth a kilogram of cure.

*

Every millimeter a monarch.

*

Give him a dekameter and he'll take a decimeter.

*

There was a crooked man, and he walked a crooked kilometer.

*

A miss is as good as a kilometer.

*

It came down like a thousand kilograms of bricks.

*

Many square meters will not make a square wise.

*

Ten milliliters, one centiliter; hundred centiliters, one litre; thousand centiliters, one kiloliter.

*

Spare the dekameter and spoil the child.

*

How many meters to Babylon?

*

A graveyard is God's hectare.

*

A cubic centimeter of sugar makes the medicine go down.

Chain Letter

Trust the Lord with all your heart, and all will acknowledge and he will light your way.

This prayer has been sent to you for good luck. The original copy came from the Netherlands. It has been around the world nine times. The luck has been sent to you. You are to receive good luck within four days of receiving this letter. It is no joke. You will receive it in the mail.

Send twenty copies of this letter to people you think need good luck. Please do not send money. Do not keep this letter. It must leave within ninety-six hours after you receive it.

A.P.S. Officer received $70,000. Dan Elliat received $60,000, but he lost it because he broke the chain. He failed to circulate this prayer. However, before his death he received $175,000, which he won.

Please send twenty copies and see what happens on the fourth day after. Add your name to the bottom of this list, and leave the top name off when circulating this letter.

Red Thinlay	A. S. Robbie	G. Mazliach
William Breedkin	Perek R. Ward	G. Jean Marie
John Ecconomistes	V. R. Stasuk	Lise V. Plouffe
C. V. Evans	T. A. Knight	D. Couture
A. Payne	Frank Davignon	S. Fortier
Donald C. Henley	W. R. Tetreault	S. Cassat
M. I. Maeen	R. F. Hider	J. Colombo

This chain comes from Venezuela, was written by St. Aptime de Cadla, a missionary from South America.

Since this chain must take a tour of the world, you must make twenty copies identical to this one and send it to your friends, parents or acquaintances and after a few days you will get a surprise. This is true even if you are not superstitious; take note of the following:

Constantine Dios received the chain in 1953. He asked his secretary to make twenty copies and send them. A few days later he won the lottery of $2,000,000.

Garlos Psandk, an office employee, received this chain. He forgot it and lost it. A few days later he lost his job. He found the chain and sent twenty copies. Nine days later he got a better job.

Zarin Berrachille received the chain. Not believing it, he threw it away. Nine days later he died for no reason.

Make twenty copies and send them. In nine days you will get a surprise.

Chain letters arrive in cycles. For three or four years, nothing; then, within a few weeks, two or three, all slightly different, all essentially the same. This one, less imaginative than many but quite typical of most, was sent by an acquaintance in November of 1973. (I failed to make my twenty copies, perhaps that explains my failure to win the Quebec Lottery.)

Great Canadian One-Liners
An Alphabet of Quotations

Kate Aitken:
A good speech should contain a lot of shortening.

Pierre Berton:
A Canadian is somebody who knows how to make love in a canoe.

James W. Curran:
Any man that says he's been et by a wolf is a liar.

Louis Dudek:
Fame — the privilege of being pestered by strangers.

Bob Edwards:
Meanwhile, the meek are a long time inheriting the earth.

Northrop Frye:
Literature is conscious mythology.

Nancy Greene:
Doesn't everyone expect to win?

Arnold Haultain:
Widows rarely choose unwisely.

George Iles:
If there were no cowards there would be no bullies.

Patricia Joudry:
Success or failure is a state of mind.

John Mark King:
God has many bests.

Sir Wilfrid Laurier:
The Twentieth Century belongs to Canada.

Jack McLaren:
Sic transit gloria Tuesday!

Alden Nowlan:
Perhaps the ultimate indignity is loneliness without privacy.

Grattan O'Leary:
There is no sense pasting wings on man unless you give him a winged nature.

Lester B. Pearson:
We prepare for war like precocious giants and for peace like retarded pygmies.

Lucien Rivard:
I'm going out to flood the rink.

Louis St. Laurent:
Socialists are Liberals in a hurry.

Israel Tarte:
Elections are not won by prayers alone.

F. H. Underhill:
A nation is a body of people who have done great things together in the past and who hope to do great things together in the future.

Stephen Vizinczey:
If our dreams aren't to be fulfilled they should at least be splendid.

W. Stewart Wallace:
In the beginning was geography.

Yevgeny Yevtushenko:
The best Canadian poet is Phil Esposito.

Robert Zend:
Being a philosopher, I have a problem for every solution.

The Last Word

The rest is silence.

Well, not quite. On his deathbed, before succumbing, W. L. Mackenzie King looked up to his nurse and said, "Thank you." And Sir Isaac Brock's dying words were (said to be): "Push on, brave York Volunteers!" And then there is the versified confession of one Cornelius Burley . . . .

The Dying Confession of Cornelius Burley
Who was Executed at London, U. Canada, on the 19th of August, 1830, for the Murder of Timothy C. Pomeroy

Oh! ye gazing spectators! be shocked at this sight,
And turn your attention to things that are right;
While BURLEY'S sad fate throughout Canada rings,
Let it teach you subjection to God and your King.

A succession of evils has stained all his life,
From degree to degree, till they ended his life;
In the merry dance, we hear him declare,
That he squandered his time, without virtue or care.

Ye sons and ye daughters of mirth and of glee,
Remember the end of CORNELIUS BURLEY;
He began in the ball-room to merrily prance,
But the gallows concluded his infamous dance.

In seducing the thoughtless, he took great delight,
And swore most profanely, as if it was right:
O, ye that delight in such vices as these,
Forsake them at once, lest your fate be like his.

The next is the Sabbath, which he did reject,
And God's holy Word he did wholly neglect:
O, ye Sabbath breakers, lay this to your heart,
And never from God's holy mandates depart.

He married a wife, when aged twenty-one;
But his inconstant heart was soon from her gone:
O, ye faithless, inconstant, and false-hearted men,
View BURLEY'S proceedings, and think on his end.

Emboldened in sin, he next, in his spite,
Takes to stealing and plunder, in shades of the night:
O, ye perpetrators of such horrid crimes,
Now shun Satan's snare, and take warning by times.

And next the cap-stone of his unholy life,
Is in shooting poor POMEROY, and taking his life;
So, now to the scaffold he's hurried along,
The rope it is fastened, and BURLEY is gone.

Now, ye wise and ye simple, ye young and ye old,
Ye rich and ye poor, who this victim behold —
You, parents and masters, and guardians of youth,
O, pity your children, and teach them the truth.

If the parents of BURLEY had taught him with care,
To avoid every evil, and shun every snare,
And the joys of religion impressed on his heart,
Perhaps, from their counsel he never would part.

Oh! parents, will you train your children with hope,
That they will avoid the disgrace of the rope;
In the nurture and wise admonition of truth,
Let their minds be impressed, in the days of their youth.

Then all you that hear of Cornelius's end,
In the strength of Christ Jesus, your lives now amend;
May the spirit of Jesus in us richly dwell —
So to this mournful subject I now bid — FAREWELL.

Cornelius Burley was the first man to be hanged in the London, Ont., area. A rare handbill was issued a month later that consisted of Burley's confession in prose and (for good measure) a second confession in verse. The authorship of the ballad is in question, for it may have been written by the repentent murderer's minister, the Reverend James Jackson, who was probably responsible for having the handbill circulated. The only known copy of this unusual item is in the London Historical Museums Division of the London Public Library.

The eccentric "Tiger" Dunlop, pioneer colonist of the London, Ont., region, even managed to speak from beyond the grave, following his death on June 29, 1848, through the medium of his justly celebrated Last Will and Testament.

The Last Will and Testament of Dr. William "Tiger" Dunlop

In the name of God. Amen.

I, William Dunlop, of Gairbraid, in the Township of Colborne, County and District of Huron, Western Canada, Esquire, being in sound health of body, and my mind just as usual (which my friends who flatter me say is no great shakes at the best of times), do make this my last Will and Testament as follows, revoking, of course, all former Wills:

I leave the property of Gairbraid, and all other landed property I may die possessed of, to my sisters Helen Boyle Story and Elizabeth Boyle Dunlop; the former because she is married to a minister whom (God help him) she henpecks. The latter because she is married to nobody, nor is she like to be, for she is an old maid, and not market-rife. And also, I leave to them and their heirs my share of the stock and implements on the farm; provided always, that the enclosure round my brother's grave be reserved, and if either should die without issue, then the other to inherit the whole.

I leave to my sister-in-law, Louisa Dunlop, all my share of the household furniture and such traps, with the exceptions hereinafter mentioned.

I leave my silver tankard to the eldest son of old John, as the representative of the family. I would have left it to old John himself, but he would melt it down to make temperance medals, and that would be sacrilege — however, I leave my big horn snuff-box to him; he can only make temperance horn spoons of that.

I leave my sister Jenny my Bible, the property formerly of my great-great-grandmother, Bethia Hamilton, of Woodhall: and when she knows as much of the spirit of it as she does of the letter, she will be another guise Christian than she is.

I also leave my late brother's watch to my brother Sandy, exhorting him at the same time to give up Whiggery, Radicalism, and all other sins that do most easily beset him.

I leave my brother Alan my big silver snuff-box, as I am informed he is rather a decent Christian, with a swag belly and a jolly face.

I leave Parson Chevasse (Magg's husband), the snuff-box I got from the Sarnia Militia, as a small token of my gratitude for the service he has done the family in taking a sister that no man of taste would have taken.

I leave John Caddle a silver teapot, to the end that he may drink tea therefrom to comfort him under the affliction of a slatternly wife.

I leave my books to my brother Andrew, because he has been so long a Jungley Wallah, that he may learn to read with them.

I leave my silver cup, with a sovereign in it, to my sister Janet Graham Dunlop, because she is an old maid and pious, and therefore will necessarily take to horning. And also my Granma's snuff mull, as it looks decent to see an old woman taking snuff.

I do hereby constitute and appoint John Dunlop, Esquire, of Gairbraid; Alexander Dunlop, Esquire, Advocate, Edinburgh; Alan C. Dunlop, Esquire, and William Chalk, of Tuckersmith; William Stewart and William Gooding, Esquires, of Goderich, to be the executors of this my last Will and Testament.

In witness whereof I have hereunto set my hand and seal the thirty-first day of August, in the year of our Lord one thousand eight hundred and forty-two.

W. Dunlop

How eloquent was Crowfoot, the great Blackfoot chief, who uttered the following words shortly before succumbing, April 25, 1890:

> A little while and I will be gone from among you, whither I cannot tell. From nowhere we came, into nowhere we go. What is life? It is a flash of a firefly in the night. It is a breath of a buffalo in the winter time. It is as the little shadow that runs across the grass and loses itself in the sunset. My children, I have spoken.

Nobility and eloquence may sometimes be caught lurking among the syllables that follow.

> JOHN DAWES
> DIED
> 1650

This inscription has been called the oldest in Canada. It comes from the burial ground, Ship Cove, Conception Bay, Nfld.

> He's done a catching cod
> And gone to meet his God

Inscription on the tombstone of an unknown sea captain, Block Island, Nfld.

> Giles is dead; peace to all liars.

From an inscription for a nineteenth-century village shoemaker, Main Cemetery, Paradise, N.S.

> Under this turf you may behold
> A lamb of God fit for the fold.

Inscribed on the tombstone of Israel Fellows who died January 26, 1788, Paradise, N.S.

> Although Boreas' blasts & Neptune's gales
> Have toss'd me to & fro,
> Yet by the Almighty God's Command
> I'm Anchored here below.

Verse on the tombstone of William Troop who died June 23, 1785, St. Paul's Cemetery, Halifax, N.S.

> What once had Virtue, Grace and Wit,
> Lies mouldering now beneath our feet.

Couplet from a tombstone common to six children of one family who died between 1772 and 1784, St. Paul's Cemetery, Halifax, N.S.

> Behold and see as you pass by,
> As you are now so once was I.
> As I am now so must you be,
> Prepare for death and follow me.

Stanza from the tombstone of James A. Holdsworth who died November 18, 1801, Loyalists' Cemetery, Digby, N.S. This is a fairly common memorial verse.

> Lord, she was thin.

Error on a tombstone from a cemetery in Annapolis County, N.S. ("Thin" should obviously be "Thine.")

> Here lies old twenty-five percent,
> The more he had, the more he lent.
> The more he had the more he craved,
> Great God, can this poor soul be saved?

Said to be the inscription on the tombstone of a nineteenth-century Nova Scotian moneylender.

> Here Lies
>
> Ezekial Aikle
> Aged 102
>
> The Good
> Die Young

Epitaph on a tombstone in the cemetery at East Dalhousie, N.S.

> It was by accident I was shot.
> To die that death it was my lot.
> The gun discharged into my right side,
> I lived five hours, then I died.

Inscription on the tombstone of Alphias Macks who died October 2, 1875, Waterside United Church Cemetery, Albert County, N.B.

> Stranger, pause a while, and view
> The last earthly tenement
> Of an honest man.

From the tombstone of Samuel Miles who died November 18, 1821, King Square Burial Ground, Saint John, N.B.

> Here lies all that remains of Charlotte,
> Born a virgin, died a harlot.
> For sixteen years she kept her virginity,
> A marvellous thing for this vicinity.

Humorous epitaph, allegedly found in a graveyard in or near Welland, Ont., 1950s.

> John Smith
> 1852-1914
> Born a Man — Died a Grocer

Alleged to be the epitaph on a gravestone "in a certain cemetery in New Brunswick."

> Ha - Ha Cemetery

Actual name of a burial place between Albert and New Horton, N.B.

> Here lies Chief Bear
> Mourned by his Relatives and Friends
> A hero who slew four of his enemies

Epitaph of an Ojibway chief, in pictographs, Lake Superior area, Ontario.

> Beloved, lovely,
> She was but seven.
> A fair bird to earth,
> To blossom in heaven.

Memorial sentiment for a child buried in 1877 at a cemetery near Picton, Ont.

> Here Lies
> General Bain
> Who Died in his Bist
> Clothes, A Rispictable
> Man — A Rayl Ould
> Irish Protestant

Inscribed on a wooden slab over the plot of the self-styled general, about 1890, Sandy Beach, Ont.

> The Beauty of this Lake of the Woods Pervades Me

From the tombstone of David K. Brown, a journalist who died at Rat Portage, October 14, 1883.

> Ye weak beware, here lies the strong,
> A victim of his strength,
> He lifted sixteen hundred pounds,
> And here he lies at length.

Verse from the tombstone of Daniel MacDonald who died on October 27, 1871 (after winning a weight-lifting contest in Montreal), Little Lake Cemetery, Peterborough, Ont.

> What is this life,
> That thoughtless wish of all?
> A drop of honey
> In a drought of gall.

Inscription on the tombstone of George Tyson who died November 29, 1857, Hamilton Cemetery, Hamilton, Ont.

> Here I lie,
> No wonder I'm dead,
> For a broad-wheeled wagon
> Passed over my head.

Allegedly an inscription from the nineteenth-century in the Ottawa region.

> I laid my wife
> Beneath this stone,
> For her repose
> And for my own.

Also said to be an inscription from the nineteenth century in an Ottawa area cemetery.

> Our Little Freddy
> Has Been Transplanted
> From This Earthly Flower Garden
> To Bloom
> In a Superior Flower Pot Above

Inscribed on the tombstone of a child, Little Lake Cemetery, Peterborough, Ont.

> Poor Emma

Another inscription from a grave in Little Lake Cemetery, Peterborough, Ont.

> If We Did Not As Brothers Live,
> Let Us Here As Brothers Lie.

Engraved over the entrance to the graveyard for Indians and Europeans at LaRonge, Sask.

> "Goodbye
> Jim
> Take ker
> O' yourself"

This once-popular line by Edgar Guest was said to be the inscription on a headstone in a cemetery near Edmonton.

SACRED TO KATIE — IPOO
SAM BOYAN HE DIDE — IPOO
RIP JULIE YECTON — IPOO
JOSEPH'S ROSIE DI — IPOO

Inscribed on wooden crosses in a West Coast Indian burial ground. Emily Carr, who recorded this eloquent inscription, explained: "Time was marked by centuries in this cemetery. Years — little years — what are they? As insignificant as the fact that reversing the figure nine turns it into the letter P."

Haine Haint

Said to be the epitaph of Arthur Haine, an avowed atheist, buried in a cemetery in Vancouver.

It is a rotten world
Artful politicians are its bane
Its saving grace is the
Artlessness of the young
And the wonders of the sky

Inscription on the tombstone of John Dean who died March 30, 1943, Ross Bay Cemetery, Victoria.

Abraham Moot
(1814 - 1903)
Atheist and Pantheist

HAS EVER SEEN IT DEMONSTRATED
THAT THE ETERNAL ELEMENTS
THAT COMPOSE EVERYTHING ANIMATE AND INANIMATE
ARE EVER CONTROLLED
BY THE IMMUTABLE LAWS OF NATURE
THAT GOVERN ALL THINGS
MATERIAL AND ETHEREAL
AND THAT THERE IS
NO CONTROLLING POWER BUT NATURE

Epitaph of a free-thinker, Lane's Cemetery, Township of Gainsborough, County of Lincoln, Ont.

> You Mariners that pass by here,
> Upon my Grave let fall a tear,
> Henry Markinson is my name,
> In the *Albion* — Captn. Hill, I came;
> 'Twas the month of April I came here,
> But did not think death was so near.

Epitaph on the tombstone of the sailor Henry Markinson who died November 30, 1850, and lies buried on Crown Prince Frederick Island, N.W.T.

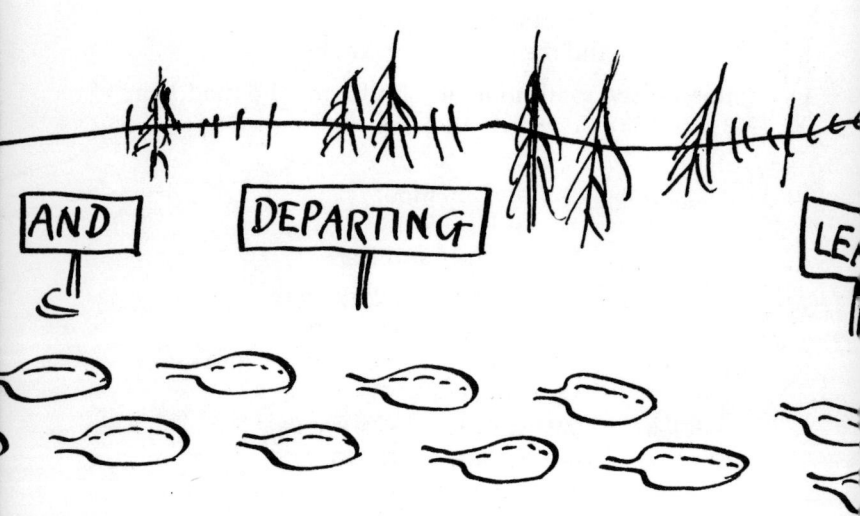

The following testament to life was found among the effects of a Canadian infantry sergeant who perished outside Ortona, Italy, on a day in December, 1943. The moving lines are frequently quoted by Farley Mowat:

> Today a bird sang for me. Today I leaned against the strong trunk of a living tree. Today a little lizard ran across my hand. So I am not alone. When I get back to Canada I'll remember this. I will cherish all of life, for all life is really one. I will never again be a destroyer, though that is what Man is. This is my dream, that we will learn to live in harmony, not between man alone, but with the whole living world.